ANNABLE'S
TREASURY
❧ OF ❧
LITERARY
TEASERS

About the Author

H. D. Annable has been a passionate reader for over eighty years. This little treasury is a natural outgrowth of his great interest in literature and history. Retired since 1965, Mr. Annable has enjoyed compiling these literary questions and quotes from his favorite works, plus condensing a few old books he felt were most important. His latest project is *A History of the Warfare of Science and Theology*, a hefty two-volume work, which is now a tidy thirty pages.

Mr. Annable also enjoys his other hobbies — book discussion groups, carpentry, and his special love, oil painting.

He and his wife live in Clinton, Connecticut.

ANNABLE'S TREASURY

~ OF ~

LITERARY TEASERS

H. D. ANNABLE

Writer's Digest Books

Cincinnati, Ohio

Annable's Treasury of Literary Teasers.
Copyright © 1989 by H. D. Annable. Printed and bound in the United States of America.
All rights reserved. No part of this book may be reproduced in any form or by any
electronic or mechanical means including information storage and retrieval systems
without permission in writing from the publisher, except by a reviewer, who may quote
brief passages in a review. Published by Writer's Digest Books, an imprint of F&W
Publications, Inc., 1507 Dana Avenue, Cincinnati, Ohio 45207. First edition.

Library of Congress Cataloging-in-Publication Data

Annable, H. D.
  [Treasury of literary teasers]
  Annable's treasury of literary teasers/H. D. Annable.
      p. cm.
  Includes index.
  ISBN 0-89879-368-8 (pbk)
  1. Literature—Miscellanea. I. Title. II. Title: Treasury of literary teasers.
PN165.A56   1989   89-34316
802-dc20   CIP

Edited by Mary Cropper
Designed by Clare Finney

To June and Carol

Introduction

How to use this book . . . viii

Introduction

Welcome to *Annable's Treasury of Literary Teasers!* We trust you are a booklover since you picked this book up. We guess also that you enjoy a good game of *Trivial Pursuit*, and always try to land on the brown space in order to answer the literature question.

This little book offers you your own private literary game. On the following pages you'll find a collection of questions, 768 "teasers" from a wide variety of literary work—novels, plays, poetry, short stories, essays, even films, musicals, and operas, contemporary and classical work alike. The range of authors is equally broad—from Socrates, Kipling, Frost and Twain to Atwood, Sontag, Koontz and Kerouac, plus many others you'll recognize as old familiar "friends" from your childhood reading days, or those you've recently added to your file of favorites.

Reading is fun and entertaining, insists H. D. Annable, the author/compiler of these questions. All his life Mr. Annable has read extensively and educated himself via great books. It was out of his love for literature that he began this book several years ago for his granddaughter. Concerned about the apparent lack of good books in her school's curriculum, Annable set out to take notes on his favorite works, compile quotes and questions, to encourage his granddaughter to share his passion. Now he wants to share that interest with you.

Annable's Treasury is divided into six sections; "Author! Author!" will test your ability to identify writers from their works or quotations; "Stage & Screen" explores movies, plays, operas, and musicals; "First & Last" looks at beginnings and endings, not just from literature but from real life, too; "Quotable Quotes" features famous and fascinating remarks; "Characters" asks you to remember those who bring stories and poems to life; and "Etc." presents a potpourri of odd and interesting items. In general, the questions increase in difficulty. For example, question six will be harder than one through five, with question seven beginning the cycle over again.

These six sections lend themselves to your own individual games with family or friends. You can, for instance, develop a lively version of *Jeopardy;* or a highly specialized *Trivial Pursuit;* or maybe an intriguing variation of *Pictionary.* And on long trips you'll want to take *Annable's Treasury* along to provide relief and diversion from the usual car games.

This little treasury is also an effective and fun way for you parents to supplement your child's school reading course; or you might want to start your own reading list at home. Likewise, teachers may find this collection a helpful addition to English or reading classes. But no matter where you choose to browse through this book, we think the questions will be just the springboard for home or class discussion on current and classical literature. And most important, *Annable's Treasury* will help expose your kids or students to the best books and encourage them to read quite naturally for pure pleasure.

For all of you lifelong bookworms and curious and casual readers young and old, wherever you are—in school, at home, at work or play—we hope that as its title suggests, this little book will tease, plus challenge, enlighten, inform—and especially offer you a good time.

Before you begin *Annable's Treasury of Literary Teasers,* we'd like to wager a little bet: That you can't read *just* one. Or two. Or three . . .

Enjoy!

Section One

Author! Author!

1. Who were the authors of the *Communist Manifesto*?

2. Name the American poet whose lesser-known works include *Legends of New England in Prose and Verse*, *Voices of Freedom*, and *Snow-Bound*.

3. Perhaps no other writer of so few works has been the subject of so many analyses. Who produced *The Catcher in the Rye*, *Nine Stories*, and *Franny and Zooey* — and few other books?

4. What American author wrote *Of Time and the River*, *The Web and the Rock*, and *You Can't Go Home Again*?

5. Can you name this Elizabethan author from the titles of two of his lesser-known works — *Sylva Sylvarum* and *New Atlantis*?

6. What German author of a very successful novel about World War I also wrote *Spark of Life* and *The Black Obelisk*?

7. *The Glass Key* and *The Thin Man* are classics of the "hard-boiled detective" school of fiction. Name the author, who is also considered the father of this style of mystery.

8. Name the English lexicographer who penned *Irene* (a play) and *Rasselas*, *Lives of the Poets*.

I *suppose I am a born novelist, for the things I imagine are more vital and vivid to me than the things I remember.*

—Ellen Glasgow

1. Karl Marx and Friedrich Engels

2. John Greenleaf Whittier

3. J. D. Salinger

4. Thomas Wolfe, who also wrote *Look Homeward, Angel*

5. Sir Francis Bacon, best known for *The Advancement of Learning* and *Novum Organum*

6. Erich Maria Remarque — his *All Quiet on the Western Front* is still a very popular anti-war novel

7. Dashiell Hammett

8. Samuel Johnson

9. What American politician who did *not* become president wrote *Call to Greatness*, *Friends and Enemies*, *Putting First Things First*, and *Looking Forward: Years of Crisis at the United Nations*?

10. Who is the author of *On Heroes, Hero-Worship, Sartor Resartus, Frederick the Great*?

11. An eighteenth-century French lawyer, philosopher, and man of letters wrote several books, including *Lettres Persanes* and *Considerations sur la Grandeur et la Decadence des Romans*. Name him.

12. Name the American philosopher and early psychologist who wrote *Pragmatism* (1907), *The Varieties of Religious Experiences* (1902), and *The Meaning of Truth* (1909).

13. What American educator whose theories continue to be very influential wrote *The School and Society* (1900) and *Democracy and Education* (1916)?

14. Which American short story writer authored "In the Midst of Life" and *The Devil's Dictionary*?

15. One of the narrative poems from *Lays of Ancient Rome* includes the lines:

    "Then out spoke brave Horatius,
    The Captain of the Gate."

    Name the nineteenth-century English biographer who composed them.

16. Identify the Scottish author who wrote *A Widow in Thrums*, *The Little Minister*, and *Sentimental Tommy*.

Wisdom *is knowing when you can't be wise.*

—Paul Engle

9. Adlai Stevenson

10. Thomas Carlyle

11. Montesquieu (Baron de la Brede)

12. William James

13. John Dewey

14. Ambrose Bierce

15. Thomas Babington Macaulay

16. James M. Barrie, who also wrote *Peter Pan*

17. What Elizabethan, known primarily as an explorer and court politician, also wrote *The Discovery of Guiana*, *The Passionate Man's Pilgrimage*, and *History of the World*?

18. What eighteenth-century French writer, famous for another work, also authored the following—*Brutus* (a play) and *Zadig*?

19. Who is the author of *Far From the Madding Crowd*, *The Mayor of Casterbridge*, and *Jude the Obscure*?

20. She wrote many books for children, including *Under the Lilacs*, *An Old-Fashioned Girl*, and *Little Men*. Name her.

21. Here are the titles of some books by an eighteenth-century French author—*The Gallant Muses*, *Discourses on the Sciences and the Arts*, *La Nouvelle Heloise*, and *Emile*. Can you name him?

22. What American religious leader published a book entitled *Science and Health* in 1875?

23. Who was the famous musician who wrote the autobiographical *Four Weeks in the Trenches: The War Story of a Violinist* (1915)?

24. Which Roman poet wrote *The Georgics* and *The Bucolics*?

I*n literature as in love, we are astonished at what is chosen by others.*

—Andre Maurois

17. Sir Walter Raleigh

18. Voltaire, whose *Candide* is better known today

19. Thomas Hardy

20. Louisa May Alcott, whose most famous book is *Little Women*

21. Jean Jacques Rousseau

22. Mary Baker Eddy

23. Fritz Kreisler

24. Virgil

25. She drew on her girlhood memories on Prince Edward Island to produce *Anne of Green Gables* and *Anne of Avonlea*. Can you name this Canadian schoolteacher and novelist?

26. Name the American anthropologist and psychologist whose works include *Coming of Age in Samoa*, *New Lives for Old*, and *Anthropologist at Work*.

27. Who is the popular American poet who wrote *The Bad Parent's Garden of Verse*, *I'm a Stranger Here Myself*, and *Everyone But Thee and Me*?

28. Name the nineteenth-century French novelist who wrote *Les Chouans*, *Illusions Perdues*, and *La Comedie Humaine*?

29. What English clergyman and political economist wrote a book in 1798 that is still used today when discussing social and economic problems? (Hint: His other works were *An Inquiry into the Nature and Progress of Rent* and *Principles of Political Economy*.)

30. This Scottish anthropologist wrote a very well-known book, but he also wrote some others along the same lines, including *Totemism* and *Folk-Lore in the Old Testament*. Can you name him?

31. Her popular romantic novels sensitively evoke earlier centuries in England. Who has given us *A City of Bells*, *Green Dolphin Street*, and *Gentian Hill*?

32. Name the author of *Black Narcissus*, *The Battle of Villa Fiorita*, and *In This House of Brede*.

A word once let out of the cage
cannot be whistled back again.

—Horace

25. Lucy Montgomery

26. Margaret Mead

27. Ogden Nash

28. Honoré de Balzac

29. Thomas Malthus — the book is *Essay on the Principles of Population*

30. James G. Frazer, whose *The Golden Bough* remains a classic

31. Elizabeth Goudge

32. Rumer Godden

33. This naturalist wrote a ground-breaking scientific treatise and *The Movements and Habits of Climbing Plants* and *Selection in Relation to Sex*. Name him.

34. A politician and noted orator, this Roman also wrote *De Senectute* (*On Old Age*), *De Amicitia* (*On Friendship*), and *De Natura Deorum* (*On the Nature of the Gods*). Who was he?

35. What prominent American woman wrote *This is My Story*, *This I Remember*, and *On My Own*?

36. Name the author of *False Entry* and *The New Yorkers*.

37. Best known of the "Beat" poets, his works have been collected into several volumes, including *Howl*, *Empty Mirror*, and *Reality Sandwiches*. He is?

38. Though he has written several highly praised novels, including *Love in a Dry Season*, he's better known for his monumental three-volume history of the Civil War (*The Civil War: A Narrative*). Who is he?

39. One of Canada's most versatile modern writers, she has produced bestselling novels such as *Surfacing* and *The Handmaid's Tale*; powerful poetry collected in works such as *The Journals of Susanna Moodie*; and insightful criticism, including *Survival*. Name her.

40. What Frenchman provoked a great deal of public controversy with a pamphlet titled *J'accuse* (*I Accuse*)?

If a poet interprets a poem of his own he limits its suggestibility.

—William Butler Yeats

33. Charles Darwin, who's more famous for *On the Origin of Species by Means of Natural Selection*

34. Marcus Tullius Cicero

35. Eleanor Roosevelt

36. Hortense Calisher

37. Allen Ginsberg

38. Shelby Foote

39. Margaret Atwood

40. Emile Zola, discussing the treason conviction of Alfred Dreyfus

41. Identify the eminent English biographer who wrote *Elizabeth and Essex*, *Eminent Victorian*, *Landmarks in French Literature*, and *Books and Characters*.

42. You've probably read at least one of this author's books in a literature course at some time. Her lesser known works are *Romola*, *The Mill on the Floss*, and *Daniel Deronda*; can you name her from these?

43. Who was the author of *The Pathfinder*, *The Deerslayer*, *The Pioneers*, and *The Prairie*?

44. Who's the midwestern poet noted for "The Raggedy Man," *The Old Swimmin' Hole and 'Leven More Poems*, and "When the Frost is on the Pumpkin"?

45. Among the works of this author are *The History of Mr. Polly*, *Outline of History*, *The Time Machine*, and *Men Like Gods*. Who was he?

46. Who wrote *The Last of the Plainsmen* and *Riders of the Purple Sage*?

47. What American novelist, journalist, and essayist wrote *Parnassus on Wheels*, *The Haunted Bookshop*, and *Where the Blue Begins*?

48. One of the foremost English orators and political thinkers wrote, among other books, *A Vindication of Natural Society*, *The Present State of the Nation*, and *Reflections on the French Revolution*. Who was this "friend" of the American Revolution?

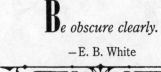

B*e obscure clearly.*

—E. B. White

41. Lytton Strachey

42. George Eliot, whose best-known works are *Silas Marner*, *Adam Bede*, and *Middlemarch*

43. James Fenimore Cooper

44. James Whitcomb Riley

45. H. G. Wells

46. Zane Grey

47. Christopher Morley

48. Edmund Burke

49. Identify the former South African lawyer who wrote *Indian Home Rule* and *Young India*.

50. What black educator wrote *Up From Slavery* and *The Story of the Negro*?

51. Name the author of *Dragon Seed*, *Pavilion of Women*, and *A Bridge for Passing*.

52. The mathematician who wrote *An Elementary Treatise on Determinants* and *Symbolic Logic* also wrote *The Hunting of the Snark* and two classic tales for a young friend. Identify him.

53. Name the author of *The Gentleman from Indiana*, *The Magnificent Ambersons*, *Alice Adams*, and *Monsieur Beaucaire*.

54. This 1651 book had the lengthy title *Leviathan; or the Matter, Forme, and Power of a Commonwealth, Ecclesiastical and Civil*. Who wrote it?

55. He's most famous for a particular spooky short story, but he also wrote *A History of New York from the Beginning of the World to the End of the Dutch Dynasty*, *Salmagundi*, and *The Legend of the Alhambra*. Can you identify him?

56. Identify the Irish satirist who wrote *The Tale of a Tub*, *The Battle of the Books*, and *A Modest Proposal*.

Choose an author as you choose a friend.

—Wentworth Dillon

49. Mohandas K. Ghandi

50. Booker T. Washington

51. Pearl Buck, best known for *The Good Earth*

52. Charles Lutwidge Dodgson, who wrote *Alice in Wonderland* and *Through the Looking Glass* under the pen name Lewis Carroll

53. Booth Tarkington

54. Thomas Hobbes

55. Washington Irving, who wrote "The Legend of Sleepy Hollow"

56. Jonathan Swift

57. This seventeenth-century diarist wrote in a private short-hand that wasn't deciphered until 1825. Who was this secretive man?

58. She's noted for both her novels and short stories, which include *Old Mortality*, *Flowering Judas* (collected short stories), *Pale Horse, Pale Rider*, and *Ship of Fools*. Identify her.

59. Name the American physician, professor, and essayist who wrote *Dissertation on Intermittent Fever in New England*, the novel *Elsie Venner*, and the poems "Old Ironsides" and "The Chambered Nautilus."

60. What English statesman was also the author of several popular novels — *Vivian Grey*, *Coningsby*, *Sybil, or The Two Nations*, *Tancred, or The New Crusade*, and *Lothair*?

61. Who is the author of *Themes and Variations*, *Lt. Schmidt*, *Safe Conduct*, and *Dr. Zhivago*?

62. Name the American author of *The Passionate Pilgrim*, *Daisy Miller*, and *The Bostonians*. His brother was a psychologist.

63. Although she's most famous for the hymn she composed during the Civil War, she also wrote *Passion Flowers*, *On Sex and Education*, and *Modern Society*. Who is she?

64. Many of the works of this American master of the short story can be found in the collections *Cabbages and Kings* and *The Four Million*. Who was he?

T*he only end of writing is to enable the readers better to enjoy life or better to endure it.*

—Samuel Johnson

57. Samuel Pepys

58. Katherine Anne Porter

59. Oliver Wendell Holmes, Sr.

60. Benjamin Disraeli

61. Boris Pasternak

62. Henry James, brother of William James

63. Julia Ward Howe (she wrote the words for "The Battle Hymn of the Republic")

64. O. Henry

65. Name the councilor of Henry VIII (later beheaded by that same monarch) who wrote *History of Richard III* and *A Dialogue Concerning Heresies*.

66. While he is most famous for his six unsuccessful presidential campaigns, this prominent socialist also wrote *The Challenge of War*, *The Great Dissenters*, *Socialism of Our Times*, and *A Socialist's Faith*. Can you name him?

67. Can you name the Russian who wrote *Notes from the Underground* and *The Brothers Karamazov*?

68. He wrote *Franklin Evans*, "When Lilacs Last in the Dooryard Bloom'd," "Song of Myself," "Song of the Open Road," and "O Captain! My Captain!" Name this man who served as a volunteer nurse during the Civil War.

69. Although he's an Australian, his best known novels, *The Devil's Advocate* and *Shoes of the Fisherman*, take place in Italy. Who is he?

70. This compact novel uses flashback and irony to tell the tragic story of three peoples' wasted lives in less than two hundred pages. Although not considered representative of this New York socialite's work, it's probably the best and most popular of her novels. What's the title and her name?

71. Identify the English author and journalist who wrote *Through the Dark Continent* and *In Darkest Africa*.

72. What Russian revolutionary wrote *The Defense of Terrorism*, *Literature and Revolution*, *My Life*, and *The History of the Russian Revolution*?

The proper and immediate object of poetry is the communication of immediate pleasure.

—Samuel Taylor Coleridge

65. Thomas More, who also wrote *Utopia*

66. Norman Thomas

67. Fyodor Dostoyevsky

68. Walt Whitman

69. Morris West

70. *Ethan Frome* by Edith Wharton

71. Henry Stanley

72. Leon Trotsky

73. Name the author of *Sister Carrie*, *The Financier*, and *The Titan*.

74. Among the works of this poet and critic are one play, *Osario*, and the poems "Kubla Khan" and "Christobel." Who was this friend of Southey and Wordsworth?

75. His philosophy expounded "reverence for life" and he won a Nobel Peace Prize. Who, better known as a medical missionary, authored *The Quest of the Historical Jesus* and *Out of My Life and Thoughts*?

76. She's the most famous practitioner of the "Had I But Known" style of mystery. Name this talented and popular novelist.

77. Which poet gave us a vivid impression of snow in "Velvet Shoes," describing it as "white down" and "silver fleece"?

78. Name the Soviet poet whose outspokenness in such poems as *Babi Yar* (commemorating the Jews killed there in World War II) and his memoirs have often caused him trouble with the Soviet authorities.

79. Some of his books are *Sebastopol*, *Anna Karenina*, and *Resurrection*. Who's the author?

80. Who is the author of *This Side of Paradise*, *The Beautiful and Damned*, *The Last Tycoon*, and *Tender Is the Night*?

Artistic growth is, more than it is anything else, a refining of the sense of truthfulness. The stupid believe that to be truthful is easy; only the artist, the great artist, knows how difficult it is.

—Willa Cather

73. Theodore Dreiser

74. Samuel Taylor Coleridge

75. Albert Schweitzer

76. Mary Roberts Rinehart (a good example of this style would be her *The Circular Staircase*)

77. Elinor Wylie

78. Yevgeni Yevtushenko

79. Leo Tolstoy, also known for *War and Peace*

80. F. Scott Fitzgerald

81. He invented the imagist school of poetry on the spur of the moment, then established it with a brilliant publicity campaign. Name the author of "In a Station of the Metro," "The Garden," "Hugh Selwyn Mauberley," and "The Cantos."

82. He wrote a book about the last campaign of a Boston politician; the title has now entered common usage as a phrase meaning a last, small triumph before a final defeat. Name the book and its author.

83. He published several critically acclaimed mystery-thrillers under the pseudonym Edgar Box in the 1950s. When later reissued under his own, more famous, name, they were less well-received. Who is he?

84. We all know Henry David Thoreau wrote *Walden*, but who wrote *Walden Two*?

85. Who wrote *The Hunchback of Notre Dame*, *Toilers of the Sea*, and *Ninety-Three*?

86. Who is the author of *The Naked and the Dead*, *Barbary Shore*, and *The Deer Park*?

87. He's considered to be one of the big three of contemporary horror fiction (the other two are Stephen King and Clive Barker). Who wrote *Phantoms*, *Strangers*, and *Whispers*?

88. The two themes of the novel *The Golden Notebook* are women's relationships with men and the author's problems with writer's block. Name the author.

A*n artist never really finishes his work;
he merely abandons it.*

—Paul Valery

81. Ezra Pound

82. *The Last Hurrah* by Edwin O'Connor

83. Gore Vidal

84. B. F. Skinner

85. Victor Hugo

86. Norman Mailer

87. Dean Koontz

88. Doris Lessing

89. Which modern French novelist and dramatist wrote *Bonjour Tristesse* when she was only eighteen?

90. Name the Spanish philosopher best known for *El tema de nuestro tempo* (*The Modern Theme*) and *La rebelion de las masas* (The Revolt of the Masses).

91. What American politician wrote *Why England Slept* and *Profiles in Courage*?

92. Who wrote *The Girls*, *So Big*, *Show Boat*, and *Cimarron*?

93. His poems, the most famous of which are "The Wreck of the Deutschland," "The Windhover," and "Vision of the Mermaids," are notable for many technical innovations such as sprung rhythm and outrides. Who was this nineteenth century Jesuit and poet?

94. His best known works are *Blood Wedding*, *Gypsy Ballads*, *Lament for the Death of Ignacio Sanchez Mejias*, and the drama *The House of Bernarda Alba*. Name this poet noted for double imagery of the real and unreal, the tragic and the comic.

95. Name the author of *The City in History* and *The Condition of Man* who helped found the Regional Planning Association of America.

96. Name the author whose witty and satirical novels include *Love in a Cold Climate* and *Don't Tell Alfred*.

I *have tried in my time to be a philosopher; but, I don't know how, cheerfulness was always breaking in.*

—Oliver Edwards

89. Francoise Sagan

90. Jose Ortega y Gassett

91. John F. Kennedy

92. Edna Ferber

93. Gerard Manley Hopkins

94. Federico Garcia Lorca

95. Lewis Mumford

96. Nancy Mitford

97. Who is the author of *A Woman of No Importance, Salome,* "The Ballad of Reading Gaol," and *The Picture of Dorian Gray?*

98. Identify the author of *A Portrait of the Artist as a Young Man* and *Finnegan's Wake.*

99. Who wrote *The Stranger, The Myth of Sisyphus,* and *The Rebel?*

100. Who wrote *Testament of Youth, Testament of Friendship,* and *Testament of Experience?*

101. What is the pen name of Emile Herzog, a famous twentieth-century French biographer, novelist, and essayist? (Hint: He's best known for his bios of Shelley [*Ariel*], Byron [*Don Juan*], and Victor Hugo [*Olympio*].)

102. He began his writing career as a journalist and film critic for the Colombian newspaper *El Espectador*. His best known work, *One Hundred Years of Solitude*, was published when he lived in Mexico. He was a resident of Barcelona when he received the Nobel Prize in literature. Name this truly international literary figure.

103. A small sampling of the work by this American cartoonist and humorist includes *Is Sex Necessary?, The Seal in the Bedroom and Other Predicaments, The Male Animal,* and *The Years with Ross.* Who's the famous Ohioan?

104. What famous essayist wrote *A Week on the Concord, A Yankee in Canada, The Maine Woods,* and *Civil Disobedience?*

One of the marks of a great poet is that he creates his own family of words and teaches them to live together in harmony and to help one another.

—Gerald Brenan

97. Oscar Wilde

98. James Joyce

99. Albert Camus

100. Vera Brittain

101. André Maurois

102. Gabriel Garcia Marquez

103. James Thurber

104. Henry David Thoreau

105. What author is best known for her book *Eichmann in Jerusalem: A Report on the Banality of Evil*?

106. This Jewish theologian has contributed to the modern development of Hasidism. Name the author of *The Prophetic Faith* and *Tales of the Hassidim*.

107. This Russian-born granddaughter of Sholem Aleichem is best known for her novel set in an American school, *Up the Down Staircase*. Who is she?

108. His series of sermons in verse, *God's Trombones*, begins with "The Creation," in which "the rainbow appeared,/ And curled itself around His shoulder." Name the poet who was also a lawyer, a principal, and a U.S. consul.

109. His work enjoyed a revival in the late 1980s after two outstanding film adaptations of his novels *A Room With a View* and *A Passage to India*. Name this author who also wrote *Howards End* and *Where Angels Fear to Tread*.

110. Her novels of the Whiteoak family of Jalna have sold over two million copies. Who is she?

111. Who wrote the hymns "Now the Day is Over" and "Onward Christian Soldiers"?

112. The popularity of his two comic novels, *Gabriela, Clove and Cinnamon* and *Dona Flor and Her Two Husbands*, has made him a folk hero in his own country. Who is this author who can find the names of his characters on everything from bars to margarine in Brazil?

I*t is the writer's privilege to help man endure
by lifting his heart.*

—William Faulkner

105. Hannah Arendt

106. Martin Buber

107. Bel Kaufman

108. James Weldon Johnson

109. E. M. Forster

110. Mazo de la Roche

111. Sabine Baring-Gould

112. Jorge Amado

113. Name the Virginian who wrote *Vein of Iron*, *The Builders*, and *The Wheel of Life*.

114. Although better known as a women's rights advocate, she also wrote fiction. Her short story, "The Yellow Wall-Paper" describes a woman's slow descent into madness. Name her.

115. Name the existentialist who wrote *The Second Sex*.

116. Although he won fame and fortune writing such rags-to-riches sagas as *Ragged Dick* and *Tattered Tom*, his life was a riches-to-rags story. Name the nineteenth-century clergyman who died in poverty despite writing one hundred enormously popular stories.

117. What's the real name of the author who published westerns, historical romances, murder mysteries, plays, and poetry under a variety of pen names? (Hint: His most famous pseudonym was Max Brand.)

118. Name the American writer and editor who produced *The Souls of Black Folk*, *Color and Democracy* and *In Battle for Peace*.

119. Who wrote the classic contemporary novel *Steppenwolf*?

120. Who has given us vivid portraits of classical Greece and Macedon in such books as *The Bull from the Sea*, *The King Must Die*, and *Fire from Heaven*?

Being entirely honest with oneself is a good exercise.

—Sigmund Freud

113. Ellen Glasgow

114. Charlotte Perkins Gilman

115. Simone de Beauvoir

116. Horatio Alger

117. Frederick Faust

118. W. E. B. Du Bois

119. Hermann Hesse

120. Mary Renault

121. Name the American poet and critic (a poetry reviewer for *The New Yorker*) whose work has appeared in *Dark Summer* and *Selected Criticism: Poetry and Prose*.

122. Who wrote:

    "When I am dead, I hope it may be said:
    His sins were scarlet, but his books were read"?

123. Who wrote the poem "The Age of Anxiety," whose title has frequently been used as a label for the twentieth century?

124. Some of his best-known poems are "Yet Do I Marvel," "A Brown Girl Dead," "Incident," and "Saturday's Child." Name him.

125. Name the author of *Wedding Day*, *His Human Majesty*, and *Generation Without Farewell*.

126. What very famous American wrote, among other things, *A Summary View of the Rights of British America*, *Notes on Virginia*, and *Life of Captain Lewis*?

127. Can you name the Italian author of *La Vita Nuova*, *De Vulgari Eloquentia*, and *De Monarchia*? (Hint: He wrote a very long, very famous poem, too.)

128. Which American president was also a scholar and the author of *An Old Master and Other Political Essays*, *The State*, *A History of the American People*, and *Constitutional Government*?

If there is a special Hell for writers it would be in the
forced contemplation of their own works, with all the
misconceptions, the omissions, the failures that
any finished work of art implies.

—John Dos Passos

121. Louise Bogan

122. Hillaire Belloc, *On His Books*

123. W. H. Auden

124. Countee Cullen

125. Kay Boyle

126. Thomas Jefferson

127. Dante Alighieri, who also composed "La Divina Commedia"

128. Woodrow Wilson

Section Two

Stage & Screen

1. Name the comedy, set in Italy, in which these characters appear—Petruchio, a no-nonsense lover; Katherina, a beautiful lady with a bad disposition; and Bianca, gentle sister of Katherina.

2. What actress suggested "Come up and see me sometime"?

3. George Kaufman did two very successful musicals with a collaborator other than Moss Hart. Despite *The Royal Family* and *Stage Door*, she is known primarily as a novelist (one of her books was set on a showboat, another in the oil fields). Who was she?

4. Name the author and the title of the play set in 1850s New England in which appear Ephraim Cabot; Abbie Putnam, his third wife; and Eben Cabot, the youngest son.

5. Name the playwright or the title of the play whose cast of characters includes Major Petkoff; his wife, Catherine; their daughter, Raina; Captain Bluntschli of the Serbian army; Sergius of the Bulgarian army; Louka; and Nicola.

6. What line follows this—"Heaven has no rage like love to hatred turned"?

7. What play set in the Samoas contains the fanatical missionaries Mr. and Mrs. Davidson, Miss Sadie Thompson, and Dr. Macphail?

8. Whose was "the face that launched a thousand ships,/And burnt the topless towers of Ilium"?

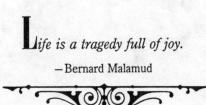

L*ife is a tragedy full of joy.*

—Bernard Malamud

1. *The Taming of the Shrew* (William Shakespeare)

2. Mae West (in the movie *Diamond Lil*)

3. Edna Ferber

4. Eugene O'Neill, *Desire Under the Elms*

5. George Bernard Shaw, *Arms and the Man*

6. "Nor Hell a fury, like a woman scorned," William Congreve (*The Mourning Bride*)

7. *Rain*, based on the Somerset Maugham short story "Miss Thompson" (John Colton and Clemence Randolph)

8. Helen of Troy (in Christopher Marlowe's *The Tragical History of Doctor Faustus*)

9. The cast of characters from this play set in nineteenth-century Norway are Torvald Helmer, his wife Nora, Mrs. Linde, Krogstad, and Dr. Rank. Name the play.

10. His style relies on Broadway slang, outrageous metaphors, and constant use of the present tense. Appropriately enough, his book *Guys and Dolls* became a hit Broadway musical. Name him.

11. In what play does Falstaff say, "The better part of discretion is valor"?

12. Name the seventeenth-century playwright who created *Every Man in His Humour, Volpone or The Old Fox, Bartholomew Fair*.

13. Name the American comic who said, "Anyone who hates children and dogs can't be all bad."

14. Who created the character who sang:

> "I'm called Little Buttercup—dear little Buttercup
> Though I could never tell why"

in *H.M.S. Pinafore*?

15. More famous for some of his other plays, he also wrote *Battle of the Angels, The Rose Tattoo*, and *Night of the Iguana*. Can you identify him from these?

16. In 1905 George Bernard Shaw wrote a play subtitled *A Comedy and a Philosophy*, which many feel was strongly influenced by the writings of Nietzsche. Which play is it?

I*'m sure if the world would blow itself up, the last
audible voice would be that of an expert saying
it couldn't be done.*

—Peter Ustinov

9. *A Doll's House* (Henrik Ibsen)

10. Damon Runyon

11. *Henry IV, Part I* (William Shakespeare)

12. Ben Jonson

13. W. C. Fields

14. William S. Gilbert

15. Tennessee Williams—his most famous works are *The Glass Menagerie* and *A Streetcar Named Desire*

16. *Man and Superman*

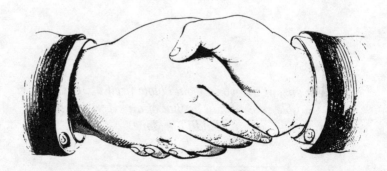

17. What three Shakespearean characters open a play with these lines:

    > "When shall we three meet again
    > In thunder, lightning, or in rain?"

    and what do actors call it instead of its title?

18. What eighteenth-century English playwright wrote, "Music has charms to sooth a savage breast"?

19. Name the sophisticated British actor and playwright of *Bitter Sweet*, *Private Lives*, *Cavalcade*, and *Pomp and Circumstance*.

20. He's one of the preeminent American playwrights of our time with eleven Obies and one Pulitzer Prize attesting to the critical acclaim he's won. Name the actor-playwright who created *Buried Child*, *Fool for Love*, and *True West*.

21. Two of the most endearing characters created for a hit Broadway play are the 81-year-old Nat Moyer and Midge Carter. What's the title of their Tony-award-winning play?

22. Can you identify the playwright of *Alcestes*, *The Trojan Women*, and *The Bacchantes*?

23. What playwright described a cynic as "a man who knows the price of everything and the value of nothing"?

24. From what play does the description of jealousy as a "green-eyed monster" come?

A series of failures may culminate in
the best possible result.

—Gisela Richter

17. The three witches, "The Scots Play" (*Macbeth*)

18. William Congreve (*The Mourning Bride*)

19. Noel Coward

20. Sam Shepard

21. *I'm Not Rappaport* (Herb Gardner)

22. Euripides

23. Oscar Wilde

24. *Othello* (William Shakespeare)

25. What play opens with the lines:

> "Two households, both alike in dignity,
> In fair Verona, where we lay our scene,
> From ancient grudge break to new mutiny"?

26. What play inspired the Cole Porter musical *Kiss Me, Kate*, which took its title from the line "Kiss me, Kate, we will be married o' Sunday"?

27. Who cried, "A horse! A horse! My kingdom for a horse!"?

28. The Maxwell Anderson / Kurt Weill musical *Lost in the Stars* was adapted from what influential novel about the effects of apartheid?

29. He wrote the plays *The Vikings of Helgoland*, *Pillars of Society*, and *An Enemy of the People*, among others. Name him.

30. The subtitle of this seventeenth-century play is *Or the World Well Lost*; what's the title?

31. This play is set in the forest of Arden. The characters are the Banished Duke, Frederick the Usurper, Oliver, Orlando, and Celia, "own cousin to Rosalind." Name the play.

32. You can probably name all the stars in *Casablanca*, but can you name the authors of the screenplay?

Our major obligation is not to mistake slogans for solutions.

—Edward R. Murrow

25. *Romeo and Juliet* (William Shakespeare)

26. *The Taming of the Shrew* (William Shakespeare)

27. Richard III (in *Richard III*, William Shakespeare)

28. *Cry, the Beloved Country* (Alan Paton)

29. Henrik Ibsen, best known for *A Doll's House* and *Ghosts*

30. *All for Love* (John Dryden)

31. *As You Like It* (William Shakespeare)

32. Julius and Philip Epstein and Howard Koch

33. Although he's most famous today for a play, in his own lifetime he was equally famous for the novel *The Sorrows of Young Werther*. Identify him.

34. Few people win Pulitzer Prizes at all, but one playwright/novelist has won one for both fiction and drama. Name the two prize-winning plays by the author of *The Bridge of San Luis Rey*.

35. Some of the works of this dramatist are *Plays Pleasant and Unpleasant*, *Three Plays for Puritans*, and *Major Barbara*. Who is he?

36. What play begins with the line "If music be the food of love, play on"?

37. What British general, who surrendered at Saratoga, was also a dramatist, creating such plays as *Maid of the Oaks* and *The Heiress*?

38. From what play does the line "Beware the Ides of March" come?

39. Beckmesser is young Walther's rival for the hand of the fair Eva Pogner in Richard Wagner's comic opera. Beckmesser is modeled on Edward Hauslick, a distinguished music critic who had annoyed Wagner by refusing to be impressed by his skill as a poet. Name the opera in which Wagner gets his revenge when Walther defeats his rival.

40. The play opens and closes with Katrin reading the beginning of her first published story. "For as long as I could remember, the house on Steiner Street had been home. . . . But first and foremost, I remember . . ." Who does she remember? (Hint: What's the title of the play?)

A free society is one where it is safe to be unpopular.

—Adlai Stevenson

33. Goethe, best known today for *Faust*

34. *Our Town* and *The Skin of Our Teeth* (Thornton Wilder)

35. George Bernard Shaw

36. *Twelfth Night* (William Shakespeare)

37. "Gentleman John" Burgoyne

38. *Julius Caesar* (William Shakespeare)

39. *Die Meistersinger von Nuremberg*

40. Mama (*I Remember Mama*, John van Druten)

41. Name the contemporary of Shakespeare who wrote the plays *Tamburlaine, The Famous Tragedy of the Rich Jew of Malta,* and *Dido, Queen of Carthage?*

42. He has given the theater some of its most vivid characters—a 1920s jazz singer, a former baseball player, a former slave, a boardinghouse owner, and a voodoo conjurer. Who is this versatile playwright who had two plays running simultaneously on Broadway in 1988?

43. In what play is the audience asked, "Do you believe in fairies? . . . If you believe, clap your hands!"?

44. Who wrote this flowery sentiment:

> "What's in a name? That which we call a rose
> By any other name would smell as sweet."

45. In what other play do the title characters of Tom Stoppard's *Rosencrantz and Guildenstern Are Dead* appear?

46. Lovers of classical music were appalled by his portrait of Mozart as an infantile, bad-mannered egotist in *Amadeus.* Who's the outrageous playwright?

47. Two of his plays, *The Duchess of Malfi* and *The White Devil,* approached the power and poetic genius of Shakespeare (others are, unfortunately, not terribly good). Who was this playwright?

48. Often compared to his contemporary, Shakespeare, the founder of modern Spanish drama produced eighteen hundred dramas, which drew their themes from collections of ballads, legends, and national traditions. Who was this prolific writer, whom Cervantes described as a "Monster of Nature"?

41. Christopher Marlowe

42. August Wilson — his plays include *Ma Rainey's Black Bottom*, *Fences*, and *Joe Turner's Come and Gone*

43. *Peter Pan* (James M. Barrie)

44. William Shakespeare (*Romeo and Juliet*)

45. *Hamlet* (William Shakespeare)

46. Peter Shaffer

47. John Webster

48. Lope de Vega

49. Among the characters in this classic modern tragedy are Willy Loman, his wife, Linda, and their sons, Biff and Happy. Name the play and its author.

50. Who said, "Something is rotten in the state of Denmark"?

51. Who won *four* Pulitzer Prizes for the plays *Idiot's Delight*, *Roosevelt and Hopkins: An Intimate History*, *Abe Lincoln in Illinois*, and *There Shall Be No Night*?

52. Who refused the Pulitzer Prize for *The Time of Your Life* because he believed commerce shouldn't patronize art?

53. The founder of *Teatro Campesino* (Farmworker's Theater) in 1965, he wrote *Zoot Suit*. Name the leading practitioner of Chicano theater in the U.S. — actor, playwright, screenwriter, and stage and film director.

54. Christopher Mahon runs away from home thinking he has killed his father. When he arrives in another county, he becomes a local hero to the people there who are impressed with his bravery. What nickname do these new friends give him (also the title of the play)?

55. *The Third Man* is best known today as a movie starring Orson Welles. Who wrote the novel on which the movie is based?

56. What character begins his famous oration with the words "Friends, Romans, countrymen, lend me your ears"?

How far that little candle throws his beams!
So shines a good deed in a naughty world.

—William Shakespeare

49. *Death of a Salesman* by Arthur Miller

50. Hamlet (*Hamlet*, William Shakespeare)

51. Robert Sherwood

52. William Saroyan

53. Luis Valdez

54. *The Playboy of the Western World* (John Millington Synge)

55. Graham Greene

56. Antony (*Julius Caesar* by William Shakespeare)

57. Which English playwright has given us *The Winslow Boy* and *Separate Tables*?

58. The rehearsal of a play is interrupted by its characters who claim they are being misrepresented by the author and the actors. In what play does this play within a play within a play occur?

59. Match each film with its writer-director:

    a. *Miracle on 34th Street*   1. John Huston
    b. *The Treasure of the*   2. George Seaton
       Sierra Madre   3. Billy Wilder
    c. *Some Like It Hot*

60. Who wrote the historical drama *Boris Godunov* (which Mussorgsky used as the basis for an opera with the same title)?

61. Who wrote *Raisin in the Sun*?

62. The characters in this play are Bassanio, Portia, Antonio, Shylock, Jessica, and Lorenzo. What play?

63. Name the playwright who crafted *The Birthday Party*, *The Lover*, *Betrayal*, and the screenplay for *The French Lieutenant's Woman*.

64. His play *Look Back in Anger* lent its name to the group of English writers now known as "the angry young men." Who's the playwright?

I *think knowing what you can not do is more important than knowing what you can do. In fact, that's good taste.*

—Lucille Ball

57. Terrence Rattigan

58. *Six Characters in Search of an Author* (Luigi Pirandello)

59. a., 2.; b., 1.; c., 3.

60. Aleksandr Pushkin

61. Loraine Hansberry

62. *The Merchant of Venice* (William Shakespeare)

63. Harold Pinter

64. John Osborne

65. What English dramatist "Finds tongues in trees, books in the running brooks, sermons in stones, and good in everything"?

66. The characters include Charlie, Charlie's younger self, Oliver, Mr. Drumm, Mary Tate (the "Yellow Peril"), Charlie's mother, and the title character—who is dead but refuses to leave Charlie alone. Name the play and the playwright.

67. The brilliant adaptation of this novel for television gave a number of performers magnificent roles in the characters of Charles Ryder, Lord and Lady Marchmain, Sebastian, Julia, and Aloysius. Name the novel and its author.

68. One of the most popular playwrights in the history of the American theater takes humorous looks at domestic problems such as getting married (*Barefoot in the Park*), getting divorced (*The Odd Couple*), and becoming middle-aged (*Last of the Red Hot Lovers*). Name him.

69. In which of Moliere's comedies of manners do Alceste, Philinte, Oronte, Celimene, and Eliante move among high society?

70. In this version of the story of Job, two circus vendors, Zuss and Nickles, don the masks of God and Satan. The Biblical "comforters" become a Freudian, a Marxist, and a Clergyman, but offer no more comfort. Who wrote the play and what is its title?

71. The famous, and often parodied, aria "Vesti la Giubba" is from what opera about an actor in the commedia dell'arte whose wife is unfaithful?

72. Although he wrote only one successful play, *Born Yesterday*, three of his screenplays for Hepburn and Tracy did very well. Who scripted *Woman of the Year*, *Adam's Rib*, and *Pat and Mike*?

65. William Shakespeare (*As You Like It*)

66. *Da*, Hugh Leonard

67. *Brideshead Revisited*, Evelyn Waugh

68. Neil Simon

69. *Le Misanthrope*

70. Archibald MacLeish, *J. B.*

71. *I Pagliacci* (Ruggiero Leoncavallo)

72. Garson Kanin (who was not credited on *Woman of the Year*)

73. What Shakespearean character said, "Who steals my purse steals trash; 'tis something, nothing . . . But he that filches from me my good name . . . Makes me poor indeed."?

74. What character in a Rostand play described himself this way: "A great nose indicates a great man—genial, courteous, intellectual, virile, courageous"?

75. By the time they won the Pulitzer Prize for *State of the Union*, this team had eight plays to its credit—seven of which had been highly successful. Name the collaborators whose works include *Life With Father* and *Anything Goes*.

76. Name the well-known critic who wrote, "The words 'Kiss Kiss Bang Bang,' which I saw on an Italian movie poster, are perhaps the briefest statement imaginable of the basic appeal of movies."

77. The title character in *The Man Who Came to Dinner* is the irascible, overwhelming, literary celebrity Sheridan Whiteside. On what real person did George Kaufman and Moss Hart base this character?

78. Which of Ionesco's plays has dialogue made up of a string of foreign language book clichés?

79. Cho-Cho-San, modeled on Nagasaki geisha Tsuru Yamamuri, is a character in what Puccini opera?

80. Name the popular lieutenant (jg) on a World War II US Navy cargo ship brilliantly brought to life by Henry Fonda in the movie with the same title.

The thing to do is to get an opera score and read that. That will bore you to death.

—Marilyn Horne

73. Iago (*Othello*)

74. Cyrano de Bergerac

75. Howard Lindsay and Russel Crouse

76. Pauline Kael (*Kiss Kiss Bang Bang*)

77. Alexander Woolcott

78. *The Bald Soprano*

79. *Madama Butterfly*

80. Mr. Roberts

81. The title character in *Come Back, Little Sheba* is rather unusual. Why?

82. Although it wasn't a musical, this movie has one of the most famous dance sequences in film history. William Holden and Kim Novak dance on a deserted dance floor lighted by Japanese lanterns. What's the title and who wrote it?

83. One of the masters of Spanish realism, he is best known in the United States for *Blood on the Sand* (1908) and *The Four Horsemen of the Apocalypse* (1916), which became vehicles for Valentino. Name the author.

84. One of the most famous lines from Shakespeare is usually misquoted as "Alas poor Yorick, I knew him well." From which play does it come?

85. This gothic novel has had several dramatic reincarnations, including a pair of famous films in which the Chaneys (father and son) each took the title role, and a spectacular musical. Name the classic horror story.

86. The movie adaptation of this novel provided Deborah Kerr (Karen), Burt Lancaster (Sargent Warden), Montgomery Clift (Prewitt), and Frank Sinatra (Private Maggio) with outstanding roles. What's the title of the novel and who wrote it?

87. Arnold Schwarzenegger made this epic character his own in the movie *Conan the Barbarian*, but what author created Conan, and in what book did the Barbarian first appear?

88. The character of Regina Giddens was created three times: once by playwright Lillian Hellman, then by actresses Tallulah Bankhead and Bette Davis. In what Hellman play does Regina appear?

81. It's a dog (the four-footed variety)

82. *Picnic*, William Inge

83. Vicente Blasco Ibanez

84. *Hamlet* (the line actually reads, "Alas poor Yorick. I knew him, Horatio")

85. *Phantom of the Opera* (Gaston Leroux)

86. *From Here to Eternity*, James Jones

87. Robert E. Howard introduced Conan in *Conan the Conqueror*

88. *The Little Foxes*

89. Although he won a Pulitzer Prize for *In Abraham's Bosom*, he's remembered more today for having invented the "symphonic drama" (*The Lost Colony*, *The Common Glory*, and *The Stephen Foster Story* are notable examples of the form). Name him.

90. Name the author of the Academy Award-winning screenplays *Butch Cassidy and the Sundance Kid* and *All the President's Men*. (Hint: He's also the writer who brought us the novels *Marathon Man* and *Magic*.)

91. In 1985, the Royal Shakespeare Company stunned the theatrical world with its brilliant adaptation of a monumental romantic novel. What was the musical (same title as the novel) and who wrote the novel?

92. The most popular miniseries in the history of television was based on what book?

93. Thanks to a movie version that starred Katharine Hepburn, *The Madwoman of Chaillot* is probably his best known work in the U.S., but his *Amphitryon 38* and *The Trojan War Will Not Take Place* are also considered classics. Name this French playwright.

94. What was the first musical to win a Pulitzer Prize and who wrote it?

95. Name the master of the Jacobean "soap opera" whose works include *'Tis Pity*, *The Lover's Melancholy*, and *The Broken Heart*.

96. Which dramatist had one of his characters deliver the classic plea of the director, "Speak the speech, I pray you, as I pronounced it to you, trippingly on the tongue"?

89. Paul Green

90. William Goldman

91. *Les Misérables*, Victor Hugo

92. *Roots* (Alex Haley)

93. Jean Giraudoux

94. *Of Thee I Sing* by George and Ira Gershwin

95. John Ford

96. William Shakespeare (*Hamlet*)

97. It takes Babe's attempted murder of her husband, Zachary, to bring the three McGrath sisters close together at last in this bittersweet comedy. Name the play and its author.

98. "It Ain't Necessarily So," "I Got Plenty of Nothin'," and "Summertime" are all songs from what classic folk opera?

99. What dramatist wrote, "The course of true love never did run smooth"?

100. One of the most dynamic showbiz duos, their hit musicals include *On The Town*, *Applause*, *On the Twentieth Century*, and *Singing in the Rain*. Name them.

101. Name the playwright who created extraordinary collections of characters in her *A Taste of Honey* and *The Lion in Love*.

102. These popular Jacobean dramatists wrote fifty plays together including *The Scornful Lady*, *The Maid's Tragedy*, and *Cupid's Revenge*. Name this dynamic duo.

103. Although he is a white South African, he is noted for his plays about blacks living under apartheid — *The Blood Knot*, *A Lesson from Aloes*, and *The Island* and *Sizwe Banzi Is Dead* (both collaborations with John Kani and Winston Ntshona). Who is he?

104. The opera *Lucia di Lammermoor* by Donizetti is based on what novel by Sir Walter Scott?

F or observe, that to hope for Paradise is to live in
Paradise, a very different thing from
actually getting there.

—Vita Sackville-West

97. *Crimes of the Heart*, Beth Henley

98. *Porgy and Bess* by George and Ira Gershwin

99. William Shakespeare (*A Midsummer Night's Dream*)

100. Betty Comden and Adolph Green

101. Shelagh Delaney

102. Francis Beaumont and John Fletcher

103. Athol Fugard

104. *Bride of Lammermoor*

105. Name the play by Jean Cocteau based on the story of Orpheus and Eurydice.

106. Who wrote *The Threepenny Opera*, *Mother Courage and Her Children*, and *The Caucasian Chalk Circle*?

107. What famous critic describes his own criticism with these words: "When I dislike what I see on the stage, I can be vastly amusing, but when I write about something I like, I am appallingly dull"?

108. Jean Anouilh updated this classic Greek tragedy to present an allegory of France under the Vichy government. What is its title (also the name of its main character)?

109. Chimene is torn between her love for the hero Don Rodrigue and duty to her late father's memory — her beloved having complicated things by killing her father in a duel. What is the title of this play set during the Spanish wars against the Moors?

110. What American showman and "Yankee Doodle Dandy" claimed July 4 as his birthdate?

111. Although he's best known as a novelist and short story writer, Ray Bradbury is also a dramatist. Which three of his own books did he adapt for the stage?

112. What is Karen Blixen's pen name, and which of her books was made into a movie starring Meryl Streep and Robert Redford?

T*he best craftsmanship always leaves holes and gaps in the works of the poem so that something that is not in the poem can creep, crawl, flash, or thunder in.*

—Dylan Thomas

105. *Orphee*

106. Bertolt Brecht

107. Max Beerbohm

108. *Antigone*

109. *El Cid* (Pierre Corneille)

110. George M. Cohan

111. *The Martian Chronicles*, *Farenheit 451*, and *Dandelion Wine*

112. Isak Dinesen, *Out of Africa*

113. *Fiddler on the Roof*, a long-running Broadway musical about a Jewish village in Russia, was based on a number of stories by a Yiddish humorist. Name him.

114. Known primarily as an absurdist playwright for *The Maids* and *The Balcony*, he was also a professional thief. Name this friend of Sartre and Cocteau.

115. Famous for her mystery novels, she also wrote *The Mouse-trap*, the longest running play in the history of London's West End. Name the "mysterious" author.

116. Name the playwright who created *The Sea Gull*, *The Three Sisters*, and *The Cherry Orchard*.

117. Name the Russian-born American composer of musicals who also wrote such popular songs and lyrics as "Blue Skies" and "White Christmas"?

118. Two sentences for acts of rebellion provided the grist for this Irish author's mill as he based several of his plays on his experiences in prison. Who wrote *The Quare Fellow* and *The Hostage*?

119. Based on the famous murder trial of Sacco and Vanzetti, this romantic tragedy ends with the deaths of doomed lovers Mio and Miriamne. Name the play and its author.

120. George Abbot, Maxwell Anderson, and Dell Andrews transformed this famous German anti-war novel into a brilliant screenplay. Although it was a pretty faithful adaptation, they did change the ending—creating a scene in which Paul is shot by a French sniper as he reaches for a butterfly. What was the title of both the novel and the movie?

113. Sholem Aleichem

114. Jean Genet

115. Agatha Christie

116. Anton Chekhov

117. Irving Berlin

118. Brendon Behan

119. *Winterset*, Maxwell Anderson

120. *All Quiet on the Western Front* (Erich Maria Remarque wrote the novel)

121. Although we learn a great deal about the two men who are expecting him, we never see the title character of Samuel Beckett's play. What's his name?

122. It's easy to remember Richard Burton and Elizabeth Taylor tearing up the screen in *Who's Afraid of Virginia Woolf?*, but can you remember the playwright's name?

123. This lyricist has given the Broadway musical some of its most memorable moments, including "Wouldn't It Be Loverly?" and Arthur's plea to remember that "one brief shining moment that was known as Camelot." Who is this lyricist?

124. Name the play and the ballet in which Theseus Duke of Athens, Hippolyta Queen of the Amazons, Bottom, Quince, Snug, Oberon, and Titania appear.

125. Name the play in which these lines appear:

> "Good night, sweet prince,
> And flights of angels sing thee to thy rest."

126. This moving tribute by a former student to Miss Cooke has challenged some of the finest actresses, including Dame Sybil Thorndyke and Katharine Hepburn. Who is the devoted student and what is the title of the play, which is set in Wales?

127. Mary tells Bob, her ex-husband, "It was hard to communicate with you. You were always communicating with yourself. The line was busy." In what play does she appear and who wrote it?

128. This handsome actor made his successful debut as a director with the adaptation of Judith Guest's *Ordinary People*. Who is he?

121. Godot (*Waiting for Godot*, Samuel Beckett)

122. Edward Albee

123. Alan Jay Lerner

124. *A Midsummer Night's Dream*

125. *Hamlet*, William Shakespeare

126. Emlyn Williams, *The Corn Is Green*

127. *Mary, Mary*, Jean Kerr

128. Robert Redford

Section Three

First & Last

1. Name the author who began a poem "Tiger! Tiger! burning bright."

2. The first line of the poem is "Oh my luve's like a red, red rose." Who wrote it?

3. What Victorian novel begins, "Whether I shall turn out to be the hero of my own life, or whether that station will be held by anybody else, these pages must show"?

4. What book written during the Italian Renaissance but still read today begins, "All States and dominions which hold or have held sway over mankind are either republics or monarchies"?

5. Who wrote the poem that begins, "Abou Ben Adhem (may his tribe increase)"?

6. This American poet, killed in action with the French army in 1916, wrote a famous poem that begins, "I have a rendezvous with death." Name him.

7. Who began his novel "There lived not long since, in a certain village of the Mancha, the name whereof I purposely omit, a gentleman . . ."?

8. The first line is "The sun shines bright in my old Kentucky home." Give the author and the title.

There's always an easy solution to every human problem—neat, plausible, and wrong.

—H. L. Mencken

1. William Blake

2. Robert Burns ("Red, Red Rose")

3. *David Copperfield* (Charles Dickens)

4. *The Prince* (Niccolo Machiavelli)

5. Leigh Hunt ("Abou Ben Adhem")

6. Alan Seeger ("I Have a Rendezvous with Death")

7. Miguel Cervantes (*Don Quixote*)

8. Stephen Foster, "My Old Kentucky Home"

9. William Faulkner began this novel with the line "From a little after two o'clock until almost sundown they sat in what Miss Coldfield still called the office because her father had called it that." Which novel is it?

10. This eighteenth-century novel begins, "In the castle of Baron Thunder-ten-tronckh in Westphalia there lived a youth, endowed by nature with the most gentle character. His face was the expression of his soul. His judgment was quite honest and he was extremely simple minded." What was its title or who was its author?

11. Name the author or give the title of the book that begins, "The fourteenth of August was the day fixed upon for the sailing of the brig Pilgrim on her voyage from Boston round Cape Horn to the western coast of North America."

12. Who penned the poem that begins, " 'Tis the last rose of summer"?

13. Who wrote, "When I wrote the following pages, or rather the bulk of them, I lived alone, in the woods, a mile from any neighbor, in a house which I had built myself."

14. Who's the author of the long poem that begins with the words, "I hear America singing, the varied carols I hear"?

15. "As I walked out on the streets of Laredo" is the first line of this poem. Name the title.

16. What classic work on economics opens with this statement: "The greatest improvement in the productive powers of labor, and the greater part of the skill, dexterity, and judgment with which it is directed, or applied, seem to have been the effects of the division of labor"?

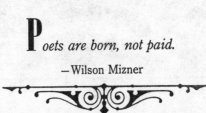

P oets are born, not paid.

—Wilson Mizner

9. *Absalom, Absalom!*

10. *Candide*, Voltaire

11. Richard Henry Dana, *Two Years Before the Mast*

12. Thomas Moore (an Irish poet, *not* Thomas More, the councilor of Henry VIII)

13. Henry David Thoreau (*Walden*)

14. Walt Whitman (*I Hear America Singing*)

15. "The Cowboy's Lament"

16. *The Wealth of Nations* (Adam Smith)

17. What 1888 utopian novel begins, "I first saw the light in the city of Boston in the year 1857. ' What!' you say, ' Eighteen fifty-seven? That is an odd slip. He means nineteen fifty-seven, of course.' "

18. "It was a feature peculiar to the colonial wars of North America, that the toils and dangers of the wilderness were to be encountered before the adverse hosts could meet." This is the opening sentence of what early eighteenth-century novel?

19. The first line of a Latin epic poem is, "Arms and the man I sing, who came from Troy." Name the author who carried Aeneas from Troy to found Rome.

20. What famous political pamphlet begins with the immortal words, "These are the times that try men's souls," and who wrote them?

21. All students of ancient history encounter the multi-volume work that begins, "In the second century of the Christian era, the Empire of Rome comprehended the fairest part of the earth, and the most civilized portion of mankind." Name the author and title.

22. Who wrote these lines:

> "She walks in beauty, like the night
> Of cloudless climes and starry skies"?

23. This long fourteenth-century Italian poem begins its journey:

> "In the midway of this our mortal life,
> I found me in a gloomy wood, astray."

Who is the author or what is the title?

24. This poem begins, "Scots, wha hae wi' Wallace bled." What is its title?

17. *Looking Backward, 2000-1887* (Edward Bellamy)

18. *The Last of the Mohicans* (James Fenimore Cooper)

19. Virgil (*The Aeneid*)

20. *The American Crisis, (no. 1)* by Thomas Paine

21. Edward Gibbon, *The History of the Decline and Fall of the Roman Empire*

22. George Gordon, Lord Byron

23. Dante, *The Inferno*

24. "Robert Bruce's March to Bannockburn" (Robert Burns)

25. "Out of the night that covers me" is the opening line of what poem?

26. "Breathes there a man with soul so dead" is the first line of what poem by Sir Walter Scott?

27. Name the German theologian who began this work with the words, "He that followeth me shall not walk in darkness, saith the Lord. These are the words of Christ and they teach us how far we must imitate His life and character, if we seek true illumination, and deliverance from all blindness of heart."

28. Whitman's poem begins with the cry, "O Captain! My Captain! Our fearful trip is done." Who is the captain to whom the poem refers?

29. This nineteenth-century anti-war poem concludes with the lines:

> "Why, that I cannot tell," said he,
> "But 'twas a famous victory."

What is its title?

30. The first line of this poem is "Pile the bodies high at Austerlitz and Waterloo." Give the title and author.

31. As he lay dying what Greek philosopher said, "Crito, I owe a cock to Asclepius; will you remember to pay the debt?"

32. What epic Russian novel begins, "Well, Prince, so Genoa and Lucca are now just family estates of the Bonapartes"? And who was the author?

For there is always this to be said for the literary profession—like life itself, it provides its own revenges and antidotes.

—Elizabeth Janeway

25. "Invictus" (William Henley)

26. "The Lay of the Last Minstrel"

27. Thomas à Kempis (*Imitation of Christ*)

28. Abraham Lincoln

29. "After Blenheim" (Robert Southey)

30. "Grass" by Carl Sandburg

31. Socrates (in Plato, *Phaedo* — "Socrates' Last Words")

32. *War and Peace* (Leo Tolstoy)

33. This Renaissance Italian work opens "DAY THE FIRST —
    As often, most gracious ladies, as, taking thought in myself,
    I mind me how very pitiful you are by nature, so often do
    I recognize that this present work will have a grievous and
    weariful beginning, inasmuch as the dolorous remem-
    brance of the late pestiferous mortality, which it beareth
    on its forefront, is universally irksome to all who saw or
    otherwise knew it." What is its title?

34. Many schoolchildren have memorized the famous poem
    that begins, "I think that I shall never see." Name the
    poem and the author.

35. Tacitus began his famous history with the words "Rome
    at the beginning was ruled by kings. Freedom and the con-
    sulship were established by Lucius Brutus." What is its
    title?

36. This book begins, "The Mississippi is well worth reading
    about." Who thought it was worth writing about?

37. The narrator of the novel begins her story, "My true name
    is so well known in the records or registers at Newgate,
    and in the Old Bailey." What is her name (the same as that
    of the novel in which she appears)?

38. What American poet, journalist and humorist wrote:

    "Let me live in my house by the side of the road
    Where the race of men go by"?

39. The first sentence of the nineteenth-century British novel
    is "A wide plain, where the broadening Floss hurries on
    between its green banks to the sea, and the loving tide,
    rushing to meet it, checks its passage with an impetuous
    embrace." Name this classic and its pseudonymous author.

40. What line follows this famous opening: "Listen, my chil-
    dren, and you shall hear"?

33. *The Decameron* (Giovanni Boccaccio)

34. "Trees" by Joyce Kilmer

35. *The Annals*

36. Mark Twain (in *Life on the Mississippi*)

37. *Moll Flanders* (Daniel Defoe)

38. Sam Walter Foss ("The House by the Side of the Road")

39. *The Mill on the Floss* (George Eliot)

40. "Of the midnight ride of Paul Revere" ("Paul Revere's Ride," Henry Wadsworth Longfellow)

41. "Bowed by the weight of centuries he leans" is the first line of this poem. What is its title?

42. This well-known book begins, "The wealth of societies in which the capitalist mode of production prevails, presents itself as an immense accumulation of commodities." Give the name of the author and the title of this book, which predicted the ultimate downfall of capitalism.

43. What poem begins with the line, "Drink to me only with thine eyes"?

44. Who composed the famous lines:

    "My country, 'tis of thee,
    Sweet land of liberty"?

45. This famous poem about the Crimean War begins, "Half a league, half a league." What is the title and who wrote it?

46. Who wrote the poem that begins, "Oh! young Lochinvar is come out of the West."

47. "In Flanders fields the poppies blow" is the first line of a poem. Who was the author?

48. "Under the shadow of Boston State House, turning its back on the house of John Hancock, the little passage called Hancock Avenue runs, or ran, from Beacon Street." Name the classic autobiography that begins with this sentence and its author.

E*very beginning is a consequence —
every beginning ends something.*

—Paul Valery

41. "The Man with the Hoe" by Edwin Markham

42. Karl Marx, *Das Kapital*

43. "To Celia" (Ben Jonson)

44. Samuel Francis Smith ("My Country 'Tis of Thee")

45. "The Charge of the Light Brigade" by Alfred,
    Lord Tennyson

46. Sir Walter Scott

47. John McCrae

48. *The Education of Henry Adams*, Henry Adams

49. We've all sung:

> "O beautiful for spacious skies,
> For amber waves of grain."

But can you name the author?

50. This nineteenth-century poem by Felicia Hemans, a staple of school recitations, begins:

> "The boy stood on the burning deck
> Whence all but he had fled."

What is its title?

51. What novel begins, "Call me Ishmael"?

52. What naturalist wrote, "For all at last returns to the sea — the beginning and the end"?

53. What eighteenth-century biography, still considered one of the greatest ever written, begins, "To write the life of him who excelled all mankind in writing the lives of others, and who, whether we consider his extraordinary endowments, or his various works, has been equalled by few in any age, is an arduous, and may be reckoned in me a presumptuous task"?

54. The first line of the poem is "I wandered lonely as a cloud." What is the title?

55. Who wrote the poem that begins, "Have you heard of the wonderful one-hoss shay"?

56. A classic eighteenth-century British novel begins, "I was born in the year 1632, in the city of York, of a good family, though not of that country, my father being a foreigner of Bremen who settled first at Hull. He got a good estate by merchandise and, leaving off his trade, lived afterward at York, from whence he had married my mother, whose relations were named Robinson." What's the title?

49. Katherine Bates ("America the Beautiful")

50. "Casabianca"

51. *Moby Dick* by Herman Melville

52. Rachel Carson, *The Sea Around Us*

53. *The Life of Samuel Johnson* (James Boswell)

54. "I Wandered Lonely as a Cloud" (William Wordsworth)

55. Oliver Wendell Holmes, Sr. ("The Deacon's Masterpiece")

56. *Robinson Crusoe* (Daniel Defoe)

57. This novel by a Civil War hero begins, "The Jebel es Zubleh is a mountain fifty miles and more in length, and so narrow that its tracery on the map gives it a likeness to a caterpillar crawling from the south to the north." Name the author or give the title of this book, which is most famous for a chariot race.

58. The first line of this poem is "A bunch of the boys were whooping it up in the Malamute saloon." Name the poem and the poet.

59. Can you name the author of the poem that begins, "The little toy dog is covered with dust"?

60. It ends with a suicide and begins, "Happy families are all alike; every unhappy family is unhappy in its own way. Everything was in confusion in the Oblonsky's house." What is the title of this tragic novel?

61. The first line of many in this long poem is "Of man's first disobedience, and the fruit." What is its title?

62. "Speak to me, Muse, of the adventurous man who wandered long after he sacked the sacred citadel of Troy." Whose adventures begin with these words?

63. The Democrats made him their presidential candidate several times because of his outstanding gift for oratory. One of his most famous speeches concludes with the ringing words, "You shall not press down upon the brow of labor this crown of thorns. You shall not crucify mankind upon a cross of gold." Name him.

64. "Hog Butcher of the World" is the unlikely first line of an ode to a famous midwestern city. Who's the poet and what city is he describing?

57. Lew Wallace, *Ben Hur*

58. "The Shooting of Dan McGrew" by Robert W. Service

59. Eugene Field ("Little Boy Blue")

60. *Anna Karenina* (Leo Tolstoy)

61. *Paradise Lost* (John Milton)

62. Odysseus (*The Odyssey*, Homer)

63. William Jennings Bryan

64. Carl Sandburg, "Chicago"

65. The sequel, *The New Chronicles of Rebecca*, picks up the engaging heroine's story after her graduation from Wareham Academy. What's the title of the first novel where we also meet her aunts Miranda and Jane, and Mr. Aladdin?

66. Name the first author to win the Pulitzer Prize for general nonfiction and the title of his account of a presidential election.

67. What novel portraying cowboy life in Wyoming is considered the prototype of the modern western? (Hint: When Trampas insults the hero, it's the first time a character says, "When you call me that, smile.")

68. Name the poem that begins:

    "Laugh and the world laughs with you;
    Weep and you weep alone,"

and its author.

69. The novel begins with this commentary on the nineteenth-century social scene: "It is a truth universally acknowledged, that a single man in possession of a good fortune must be in want of a wife." Give the author and the title.

70. "It was the best of times, it was the worst of times." Who wrote these words in what novel?

71. Which is the title of Vonnegut's first novel: *Mother Night*, *Cat's Cradle*, *Player Piano*, or *Slaughterhouse Five*?

72. Great things may come from small beginnings. A short story about a boy and his horse became a novel, the novel led to a sequel titled *Thunderhead*, and both novels were made into successful motion pictures. What is the title of the original short story?

65. *Rebecca of Sunnybrook Farm* (Kate Douglas Wiggin)

66. Theodore H. White, *The Making of the President, 1960*

67. *The Virginian* (Owen Wister)

68. "Solitude" by Ella Wheeler Wilcox

69. Jane Austen, *Pride and Prejudice*

70. Charles Dickens, *A Tale of Two Cities*

71. *Player Piano*

72. *My Friend Flicka* (Mary O'Hara)

73. This Pulitzer-Prize-winning novel about loss and self-discovery ends with "The last thing Laurel saw, before they whirled into speed, was the twinkling of their hands, the many small and unknown hands, wishing her goodbye." Name the novel and its author.

74. She wrote, "When I am dead my dearest, / Sing no sad songs for me," but in an excess of grief he buried all his literary output with her (and had to dig it back up again later). Who was this pre-Raphaelite couple?

75. The poem begins, "It is an ancient Mariner." Name the author.

76. What poet began one of his most famous works with "Whose woods these are I think I know"?

77. What's the title of Bernard Malamud's first novel? (Hint: It made a great movie starring Robert Redford.)

78. What's the title of Thomas Mann's first novel—the one about the decline of a prosperous German family?

79. This brilliant modernist poet is noted for swift, unexpected associations, comparisons, and distinctions underlaid by a very fine morality. The final couplet of her anti-war poem, "In Distrust of Merits" is a good example of this:

> "Beauty is everlasting
> and dust is for a time."

Who is she?

80. Who was the first editor of *Poetry: A Magazine of Verse*, one of the first "little" magazines and part of the Chicago Renaissance?

*If I didn't know the ending of a story, I wouldn't begin.
I always write my last line, my last paragraph,
my last page first.*

—Katherine Anne Porter

73. *The Optimist's Daughter* by Eudora Welty

74. Christina and Dante Gabriel Rossetti

75. Samuel Taylor Coleridge ("The Rime of the Ancient Mariner")

76. Robert Frost ("Stopping by the Woods on a Snowy Evening")

77. *The Natural*

78. *Buddenbrooks*

79. Marianne Moore

80. Harriet Moore

81. What, according to Isaac Asimov, is the first law of robotics?

82. Name the book that ends, "He had won the victory over himself. He loved Big Brother," and its author.

83. Can you identify the author and title of this novel from its first sentence? "Buck did not read the newspapers, or he would have known that trouble was brewing, not alone for himself, but for every tidewater dog strong of muscle and with the warm, long hair from Puget Sound to San Diego."

84. Who ran a very popular nineteenth-century "ladies' magazine," helped establish Mother's Day as a holiday, and began a poem with "Mary had a little lamb"?

85. Who received both critical and popular acclaim for her first novel, *Penhally*, the story of three generations on a Kentucky plantation?

86. Although "It was a dark and stormy night" is now Snoopy's favorite way to begin a book, two authors have already used it to begin their novels. Who are they and what did they write?

87. In reference to another kind of ending, who said, "Old soldiers never die; they just fade away"?

88. A World War I ambulance driver based a novel on his wartime experiences. It closes with these words: "It was like saying goodbye to a statue. After a while I went out and left the hospital and walked back to the hotel in the rain." Name the novel and its author.

W*e spend our time envying people whom we wouldn't like to be.*

—Jean Rostand

81. "A robot may not injure a human being, or, through inaction, allow a human being to come to harm." See *I, Robot* for the rest of the laws.

82. *1984* by George Orwell

83. *Call of the Wild*, Jack London

84. Sarah Josepha Hale

85. Caroline Gordon

86. Madeleine L'Engle in *A Wrinkle in Time* and Edward George Earle Bulwer-Lytton in *Paul Clifford*

87. Douglas MacArthur

88. *A Farewell to Arms*, Ernest Hemingway

89. In the introduction to her book of poems, *Spin a Soft Black Song*, she wrote, "You could say we've lost our innocence. That's a little worse than losing the nickel to put in Sunday school, though not quite as bad as losing the dime for ice cream afterward." Who is she?

90. John Fowles is well-known today for *The French Lieutenant's Woman*, but what was the title of his first novel?

91. Who wrote the famous quatrain that begins, "I never saw a purple cow"?

92. Who wrote the poem that begins:

> "When I am dead and over me bright April
> shakes out her rain-drenched hair"?

93. The poem begins:

> "The fog comes in
> on little cat feet."

Who's the poet?

94. "The subject of this Essay is not the so-called Liberty of the will, so unfortunately opposed to the misnamed doctrine of Philosophical Necessity; but Civil or Social Liberty." Which of John Stuart Mill's books begins with these words?

95. The sensitive story of an overweight girl who hates gym class begins, "I hate my father." Name the book.

96. Who is considered to be the first *English* author of detective and mystery novels?

I t is the province of knowledge to speak
and it is the privilege of wisdom to listen.

—Oliver Wendell Holmes

89. Nikki Giovanni

90. *The Collector*

91. Gelett Burgess

92. Sara Teasdale

93. Carl Sandburg ("Fog")

94. *On Liberty*

95. *The Cat Ate My Gym Suit* (Paula Danziger)

96. Wilkie Collins (*The Moonstone* and *The Woman in White*)

97. Which Saki story about a young man with a nervous condition, an imaginative young woman, and a "lost" hunting party ends, "Romance at short notice was her specialty."

98. "I still have a piece of that root, put away in a box with my journal, my can of tobacco tags, the newspaper write-up when I got run over by the train, a photograph of me and Miss Love and Grandpa in the Pierce, my Ag College diploma from the University — and the buckeye that Lightfoot gave me." With these words the narrator ends his story in what novel? And who's the author?

99. This epic poem begins, "This is the forest primeval. The murmuring pines and the hemlocks . . . Stand like druids of old." Give the title and its author.

100. This historic document ends with the following oath: "And for the support of this Declaration, with a firm reliance on the Protection of Divine Providence, we mutually pledge to each other our Lives, our Fortunes and our sacred Honor." What is it?

101. What novel begins, "Now I am thirteen, but when I was a chile, it was hard to be a chile because my block is a tough block and my school is a tough school"?

102. Give the title of James Baldwin's first novel, which tells of a fourteen-year-old boy's religious awakening.

103. You know the poem that begins:

> "Over the river and through the wood,
> To grandfather's house we go,"

but do you know who wrote it?

104. It began with a phone call at nine a.m. on June 17, 1972. By the time it had ended, a president faced possible impeachment. What major event in American history was it?

97. "The Open Window"

98. *Cold Sassy Tree*, Olive Ann Burns

99. "Evangeline," Henry Wadsworth Longfellow

100. The Declaration of Independence (Thomas Jefferson)

101. *A Hero Ain't Nothin' But a Sandwich* (Alice Childress)

102. *The Fire Next Time*

103. Lydia Maria Child ("Thanksgiving Day")

104. The Watergate investigation by Robert Woodward and Carl Bernstein (*All the President's Men*)

105. " 'Where's Papa going with that ax?' said Fern to her mother as they were setting the table for breakfast" is the first line of a classic children's story by E. B. White. What's the title?

106. What was the title of Jean Auel's first novel?

107. *A Few Green Leaves* may be seen as the culmination of this author's work. Who brought together the setting of her first novel and many characters and themes from later ones in her last book?

108. In what novel did Albert Campion begin his career as a detective (the first of twenty-one such cases)?

109. What is the title of Margaret Drabble's first novel? It's about a young woman just graduated from Oxford who draws on the experiences of her sister and her friends to sort out her own approach to life.

110. Which of Joan Didion's books begins, "We tell ourselves stories in order to live. . . . We interpret what we see, select the most workable of the multiple choices. We live entirely, especially if we are writers, by the imposition of a narrative line upon disparate images, by the 'ideas' with which we have learned to freeze the shifting phantasmagoria which is our actual experience"?

111. Name the title and the author of the book that begins, "There's a tree that grows in Brooklyn. Some people call it the Tree of Heaven. No matter where its seed falls, it makes a tree which struggles to reach the sky."

112. The theme of this somber novel is summed up in its final words: "Ralph wept for the end of innocence, the darkness of man's heart, and the fall through the air of the true, wise friend called Piggy." What's its title?

105. *Charlotte's Web*

106. *The Clan of the Cave Bear*

107. Barbara Pym

108. *The Crime at Black Dudley* by Margery Allingham

109. *A Summer Bird-Cage*

110. *The White Album*

111. *A Tree Grows in Brooklyn*, Betty Smith

112. *Lord of the Flies* (William Golding)

113. *The Bourne Supremacy* was Robert Ludlum's first sequel. What's the title of the first novel?

114. Which of Helen MacInnes's novels begins with this description of an Austrian lake? "The lake was cold, black, evil, no more than five hundred yards in length, scarcely two hundred in breadth, a crooked stretch of glassy calm shadowed by the mountainsides that slipped steeply into dark waters and went plunging down."

115. Tax reform has been a major theme of American political writing from the very beginning. Name the economist and reformer whose book *Progress and Poverty*, advocating tax simplification (a single tax based on land) began, "Reducing to its most compact form the problem we have set out to investigate, let us examine, step by step, the explanation which political economy, as now accepted by the best authority, gives of it."

116. One of the greatest poems of the modernist period begins with the words, "April is the cruellest month." Name the author and the title of this poem which uses images of the desert and the modern city as metaphors.

117. Who wrote the poem that begins:

    "in Just-
    spring when the world is mud-
    luscious . . . "?

118. What series of books written by a British prime minister ends with the words, "It only remains for me, to express to the British people, for whom I have acted in these perilous years, my profound gratitude for the unflinching, unswerving support which they have given me during my task, and for the many expressions of kindness which they have shown toward their servant."

119. A long succession of bestsellers for what author began with *Dynasty of Death*? (Hint: She also wrote *Captains and the Kings*.)

120. In the famous Abbott and Costello routine, who's on first?

113. *The Bourne Identity*

114. *The Salzburg Connection*

115. Henry George

116. *The Waste-Land* by T. S. Eliot

117. e. e. cummings ("Chansons Innocentes")

118. *The Second World War* by Winston Churchill

119. Taylor Caldwell

120. *Who*, of course!

121. What's the title of the first book of *The Chronicles of Narnia*?

122. Who wrote the poem that begins:

"The Owl and the Pussy-Cat went to sea
In a beautiful pea-green boat"?

123. "One Christmas was so much like another, in those years around the seatown corner now and out of all sound except the distant speaking of the voices I sometimes hear a moment before sleep, that I can never remember whether it snowed for six days and six nights when I was twelve or whether it snowed for twelve days when I was six." So begins a collection of Christmas memories. Whose memories, and what title did he give it?

124. What was Peter Benchley's first novel?

125. What's the title of the first volume of the Dragonriders of Pern series?

126. Who wrote the classic feminist novel that begins, "Mira was hiding in the ladies' room. She called it that, even though someone had scratched out the word *ladies'* in the sign on the door, and written *women's* underneath"?

127. The last book in this trilogy has "The Wishsong" in its title. What's the title of the first book?

128. Who wrote the poem that begins, "If you can keep your head when all about you/are losing theirs." What is its title?

Happiness is a how, not a what;
a talent, not an object.

—Hermann Hesse

121. *The Lion, the Witch, and the Wardrobe* (C. S. Lewis)

122. Edward Lear ("The Owl and the Pussy-Cat")

123. *A Child's Christmas in Wales* by Dylan Thomas

124. *Jaws*

125. *Dragonflight* (Ann McCaffrey)

126. Marilyn French, *The Women's Room*

127. *The Sword of Shannara* (Terry Brooks)

128. Rudyard Kipling ("If")

Quotable Quotes

1. Who wrote, "The best laid schemes o' mice and men/Gang aft a-gley"?

2. Whose raven "quoth 'Nevermore' "?

3. What famous line of sonnet precedes "Thou art more lovely and more temperate"?

4. Who wrote:

> "Alone, alone, all, all alone,
> Alone on a wide, wide sea!"?

5. Who wrote the lines:

> "Twinkle, twinkle, little star,
> How I wonder what you are"?

6. What American poet wrote of Columbus:

> "He gained a world, he gave that world
> Its grandest lesson: 'On! Sail on!' "?

7. In what poem does the line "One if by land, and two if by sea" appear?

8. Complete the line of poetry that begins, "A thing of beauty ..."

I have lived by my wits all my life and I thank the Lord they are still in one, whole piece. I don't need glasses, Benzedrine, or a psychiatrist.

—Elsa Maxwell

1. Robert Burns ("To a Mouse")

2. Edgar Allen Poe's ("The Raven")

3. "Shall I compare thee to a summer's day?" (William Shakespeare, "Sonnet 3")

4. Samuel Taylor Coleridge ("The Rime of the Ancient Mariner")

5. Jane and Ann Taylor

6. Joaquin Miller ("Columbus")

7. "Paul Revere's Ride" (Henry Wadsworth Longfellow)

8. "A thing of beauty is a joy forever" ("Endymion" by John Keats)

9. What American journalist wrote:

> "Men seldom make passes
> At girls who wear glasses"?

10. What German religious reformer wrote, "A mighty fortress is our God"?

11. Who wrote, "Be it ever so humble, there's no place like home"?

12. Name the Latin poet who wrote, "The mountain labors and gives birth to a mouse."

13. "Genius is one percent inspiration and ninety-nine percent perspiration." What American inventor said this?

14. Who wrote:

> "Fifteen men on the Dead Man's Chest
> Yo-ho-ho, and a bottle of rum!"?

15. Who wrote:

> "Full many a flower is born to blush unseen
> And waste its sweetness on the desert air"?

16. What religious leader defended himself with the words, "Here I stand, I cannot do otherwise"?

A *new question has arisen in modern man's mind, the question, namely, whether life is worth living . . . No sensible answer can be given to the question . . . because the question does not make any sense.*

—Erich Fromm

9. Dorothy Parker

10. Martin Luther

11. John Howard Payne ("Home, Sweet Home")

12. Horace (*Epistles, Book III [Ars poetica]*)

13. Thomas Edison (*Life*)

14. Robert Louis Stevenson (*Treasure Island*)

15. Thomas Gray ("Elegy Written in a Country Churchyard")

16. Martin Luther (at the Diet of Worms, April 18, 1521)

17. What early twentieth-century journalist wrote, " 'Oh well,' said Mr. Hennessy, 'we are as the Lord made us.' 'No,' said Mr. Dooley, 'lave us be fair. Lave us take some iv th' blame oursilves' "?

18. In what poem are these lines found:

    "Tell me not, in mournful numbers,
    Life is but an empty dream!"?

19. What baseball manager said, "Nice guys finish last"?

20. Who "never met a man I didn't like"?

21. In which of his speeches did Abraham Lincoln say, "With malice toward none, with charity for all, with firmness in the right"?

22. Who faced execution bravely, saying, "Patriotism is not enough"?

23. What seventeenth-century English poet gave us:

    "Stone walls do not a prison make,
    Nor iron bars a cage"?

24. From what poem does the expression "Death, be not proud" come, and who is the author?

Great imaginations are apt to work from hints and suggestions, and a single moment of emotion is sometimes sufficient to create a masterpiece.

—Margaret Sackville

17. Finley Peter Dunne (*Newport*)

18. "A Psalm of Life" (Henry Wadsworth Longfellow)

19. Leo Durocher

20. Will Rogers

21. The Second Inaugural Address

22. Edith Cavell

23. Richard Lovelace ("To Althea")

24. "Death" by John Donne

25. Caesar sent the message "Veni, vidi, vinci" to Rome to announce what achievement?

26. Finish the lines of poetry that begin with the words "My candle burns . . ."

27. What poet wrote:

    "I'se still climbin',
    And life for me ain't been no crystal stair"?

28. To whom was Churchill referring when he said, "Never in the field of human conflict was so much owed by so many to so few"?

29. "There is only one thing worse than being talked about, and that is not being talked about." From what novel does this come, and who wrote it?

30. What philosophy is associated with "It is impossible to live pleasurably without living wisely, well, and justly, and impossible to live wisely, well and justly without living pleasurably"?

31. What stands "under the spreading chestnut tree"?

32. What did Wynken, Blynken, and Nod do one night?

Friendship of a kind that cannot easily be reversed tomorrow must have its roots in common interests and shared beliefs, and even between nations, in some personal feeling.

—Barbara Tuchman

25. A military victory in Dacia (Suetonius, *Lives of the Caesars*)

26. "My candle burns at both ends;
    It will not last the night."
    (From "First Fig," *A Few Figs from Thistles*, Edna St. Vincent Millay)

27. Langston Hughes ("Mother to Son")

28. The Royal Air Force

29. *The Picture of Dorian Gray* by Oscar Wilde

30. Epicurean (quote from Epicurus appears in Diogenes Laertius, *Lives of Eminent Philosophers, book 10*)

31. The village smithy ("The Village Blacksmith" by Henry Wadsworth Longfellow)

32. "Sailed off in a wooden shoe" ("Wynken, Blynken, and Nod," Eugene Field)

33. "The study of the art of motorcycle maintenance is really a miniature study of the art of rationality itself. Working on a motorcycle, working well, caring, is to become part of a process, to achieve an inner peace of mind." This is the theme of what book, and who wrote it?

34. "The logic of the Cistercian life was, then, the complete opposite to the logic of the world, in which men put themselves forward, so that the most excellent is the one who stands out, the one who is eminent above the rest, who attracts attention." Name the author of this quote from *The Seven Storey Mountain*.

35. We all know the lines:

> "Praise God, from whom all blessings flow,
> Praise Him, all creatures here below."

But who wrote them?

36. A prominent American journalist wrote, "Puritanism is the haunting fear that someone, somewhere, may be happy." Name him.

37. According to the poem "Locksley Hall," what happens to a young man in spring?

38. On whose desk was the sign "The buck stops here"?

39. What military leader believed, "You write to me that it's impossible; the word is not French"?

40. In what poem did W. B. Yeats suggest these words for his tombstone:

> "Cast a cold eye
> On life, on death,
> Horseman, pass by!"?

An honest man's the noblest work of God.

—Alexander Pope

33. *Zen and the Art of Motorcycle Maintenance* by Robert M. Pirsig

34. Thomas Merton

35. Bishop Thomas Ken ("Doxology," *Morning and Evening Hymns*)

36. H. L. Mencken ("Sententiae," *A Book of Burlesques*)

37. His fancy turns lightly to love (Alfred, Lord Tennyson)

38. Harry Truman

39. Napoleon Bonaparte (letter to General Lemarois, July 19, 1813)

40. "Under Ben Bulben," and they are actually inscribed there!

41. John Masefield wrote, "I must down to the seas again, to the lonely sea and the sky" in what poem?

42. Who declared:

   "Oh, East is East, and West is West,
   And never the twain shall meet"?

43. What famous shy person wrote, "I'm Nobody! Who are you?/Are you—Nobody—too?"?

44. What line of poetry follows "For of all sad words of tongue or pen"?

45. Who said, "Don't look back. Something may be gaining on you"?

46. Who described the retreat from Moscow as moving "from the sublime to the ridiculous"?

47. Whose motto was to "pray for the dead and fight for the living"?

48. What is the title of the poem with these lines:

   "Back, turn backward, O Time in your flight,
   Make me a child again, just for tonight!"?

M emory is a great betrayer.

—Anais Nin

41. "Sea Fever"

42. Rudyard Kipling ("The Ballad of East and West")

43. Emily Dickinson

44. "The saddest words are these, 'It might have been' " (John Greenleaf Whittier, "Maud Muller")

45. Leroy (Satchel) Paige

46. Napoleon Bonaparte

47. Mother Jones

48. "Rock Me to Sleep, Mother" (Elizabeth Allen)

49. What line follows "The woods are lovely, dark and deep"?

50. Where do the lines:

> "A Book of Verses underneath the Bough,
> A Jug of Wine, a Loaf of Bread—and Thou"

come from?

51. What English poet wrote:

> "More things are wrought by prayer
> Than this world dreams of"?

52. What caustic Anglo-Irish writer turned an old proverb upside down, writing "Lack of money is the root of all evil"?

53. Who wrote, "I am monarch of all I survey"?

54. Name the Irish poet who wrote, "The harp that once through Tara's halls."

55. Who is the author of these lines:

> " 'Twas brillig, and the slithy toves
> Did gyre and gimble in the wabe"?

56. Who said, "Ask not what your country can do for you; ask what you can do for your country"?

Some books are to be tasted, others to be swallowed, and some few to be chewed and digested; that is, some books are to be read only in parts; others to be read but not curiously; and some few to be read wholly, and with diligence and attention.

—Sir Francis Bacon

49. "But I have promises to keep" (Robert Frost, "Stopping by the Woods on a Snowy Evening")

50. *The Rubiyat of Omar Khayyam*

51. Alfred, Lord Tennyson (*Morte d'Arthur*)

52. George Bernard Shaw (*Man and Superman, Maxims for Revolutionists*)

53. William Cowper ("The Solitude of Alexander Selkirk")

54. Thomas Moore

55. Lewis Carroll (*Alice in Wonderland*)

56. John F. Kennedy (Inaugural Address, January 20, 1961)

57. "Caesar had his Brutus, Charles the First his Cromwell, and George the Third" [here the speech was interrupted by cries of "Treason!"] "may profit by their example. If this be treason, make the most of it." Who delivered the speech and who interrupted it?

58. What nineteenth-century Scottish novelist and poet ruefully noted:

> "Oh, what a tangled web we weave,
> When first we practice to deceive'?

59. What American politician said, "What this country needs is a good five-cent cigar"?

60. Who wrote:

> "Ah, but a man's reach should exceed his grasp
> Or what's a heaven for"?

61. Who wrote, "Mine eyes have seen the glory of the coming of the Lord"?

62. Give the famous line of poetry that precedes "Let me count the ways."

63. Who said, "If you can't stand the heat, get out of the kitchen"?

64. Which character in *Alice's Adventures in Wonderland* said, "The time has come to talk of many things"?

P oetry is the spontaneous overflow of powerful
feelings; it takes its origin from emotion
recollected in tranquility.

—William Wordsworth

57. Patrick Henry delivered it with the interruption from the Speaker of Virginia's House of Burgesses

58. Sir Walter Scott (*Marmion*)

59. Thomas Marshall

60. Robert Browning (*Andrea del Sarto*)

61. Julia Ward Howe ("The Battle Hymn of the Republic")

62. "How do I love thee?" (Elizabeth Barrett Browning, Sonnet 43, *Sonnets from the Portugese*)

63. Harry Truman

64. The Walrus

65. What line follows "Once to every man and nation comes the moment to decide"?

66. Where do we find this sage advice: "Early to bed and early to rise, makes a man healthy, wealthy, and wise"?

67. "I know not what course others may take but as for me, give me liberty or give me death!" Who said it?

68. What did the dog do in the nighttime in "Silver Blaze"?

69. Who announced from London, "Reports of my death are greatly exaggerated"?

70. What line of poetry follows "Here once the embattled farmers stood"?

71. Name the ancient scientist who said, "Give me where to stand, and I will move the earth [with a lever]."

72. What German philosopher said, "I teach you the Superman. Man is something that is to be surpassed"?

As for Doing-good, that is one of the professions which are full. Moreover, I have tried it fairly, and, strange as it may seem, am satisfied that it does not agree with my constitution.

—Henry David Thoreau

65. "In the strife of Truth with Falsehood, for the good or evil side" (James Russell Lowell, "The Present Crisis")

66. In *Poor Richard's Almanac* (Benjamin Franklin)

67. Patrick Henry

68. "The dog did nothing in the nighttime" (Arthur Conan Doyle)

69. Mark Twain

70. "And fired the shot heard round the world" (Ralph Waldo Emerson, "Concord Hymn")

71. Archimedes ("Pappus of Alexandria," *Collectio Book II, prop. 10*)

72. Friedrich Nietzsche (*Thus Spake Zarathustra*)

73. Who wrote, "No man is an island"?

74. Who did Virgil advise fearing, "even though they come bearing gifts"?

75. What line of poetry follows "I could not love thee, Dear, so much"?

76. What eighteenth-century critic wrote, "To err is human, to forgive divine"?

77. Who wrote that "memory is a great betrayer"?

78. Who wrote that "hope springs eternal in the human breast"?

79. Who convinced Depression-torn America that "the only thing we have to fear is fear itself"?

80. Who began his description of Gaul with these words: "All Gaul is divided into three parts . . ."?

I *expect to pass through life but once. If therefore, there be any kindness I can show, or any good thing I can do to any fellow being, let me do it now, and not defer or neglect it, as I shall not pass this way again.*

—William Penn

73. John Donne (*Holy Sonnets*)

74. The Greeks (*The Aeneid*)

75. "Loved I not honor more" (Richard Lovelace, "To Lucasta: Going to the Wars")

76. Alexander Pope (*An Essay on Criticism, Part II*)

77. Anais Nin (*The Diary of Anais Nin*)

78. Alexander Pope (*An Essay on Man*)

79. Franklin D. Roosevelt (First Inaugural Address, March 4, 1933)

80. Julius Caesar (*De Bello Gallico I, 1*)

81. "All hope abandon, ye who enter here" marks the entrance to Hell in what literary classic?

82. What optimistic poet wrote, "God's in His heaven—All's right with the world"?

83. What does it take to make a house a home according to Edgar Guest?

84. Name the poet who coined the phrase "ships that pass in the night."

85. "When all at once I saw a crowd,
    A host of golden daffodils."

    Who's the poet?

86. A little what is "a dangerous thing"?

87. "Where ignorance is bliss, / 'Tis folly to be" what?

88. What poem includes the line "Come live with me and be my love," and who wrote it?

The great tragedy of science—the slaying of a beautiful hypothesis by an ugly fact.

—Thomas Huxley

81. Dante's *Inferno*

82. Robert Browning ("Pippa Passes")

83. "It takes a heap o' livin' in a house t' make it home" ("Home")

84. Henry Wadsworth Longfellow ("The Theologian's Tale")

85. William Wordsworth ("I Wandered Lonely as a Cloud")

86. "Learning" (at least according to Alexander Pope in *An Essay on Criticism*)

87. "Wise" (according to Thomas Gray in *On a Distant Prospect of Eton College*)

88. Christopher Marlowe, "The Passionate Shepherd to His Love"

89. Who observed that "the Colonel's Lady and Judy O'Grady/ Are sisters under their skins!"?

90. Who said, "Whatever women do they must do twice as well as men to be thought half as good. Luckily, this is not difficult."

91. This often parodied line, "For I'm to be queen of the May, mother, I'm to be queen o' the May" comes from a ballad. Who wrote this tale of a heartless village beauty?

92. The fox's secret is very simple. "It is only with the heart that one can see rightly; what is essential is invisible to the eye." Who wrote the classic story in which this line appears?

93. Who wrote, "The medium is the message because it is the medium that shapes and controls the search," in his groundbreaking book on mass communication?

94. Can you name the Hindu poet, novelist, musician, playwright, and artist who wrote, "Pleasure is frail like a dewdrop. While it laughs it dies"?

95. Who wrote:

> "In the sun that is young once only,
> Time let me play and be
> Golden in the mercy of his means"?

96. Who described the role and function of the critic as "the aim of all commentary on art now should be to make works of art — and, by analogy, our own experiences — more, rather than less, real to us. The function of criticism should be to show *how it is what it is*, even *that it is what it is*, rather than to show *what it means*"?

L*ook to this day!*
For it is life, the very life of life.

—Attributed to Kalidasa, Hindu poet

89. Rudyard Kipling ("The Ladies")

90. Charlotte Whitton (quoted in *Canada Month*, June, 1963)

91. Alfred, Lord Tennyson ("The May Queen")

92. Antoine St. Exupery (*The Little Prince*)

93. Marshall McLuhan

94. Rabindranath Tagore

95. Dylan Thomas (*Fern Hill*)

96. Susan Sontag (*Against Interpretation*)

97. In *Gift from the Sea* she wrote, "Perhaps middle-age is, or should be, a period of shedding shell; the shell of ambition, the shell of material accumulations and possessions, the shell of the ego." Name her.

98. Who described his generation as "the beat generation"?

99. Who had "a dream that one day on the red hills of Georgia, the sons of former slaves and the sons of former slave owners will be able to sit together at the table of brotherhood . . ."?

100. Name the English mathematician and philosopher who observed that "The degree of one's emotion varies inversely with one's knowledge of the facts — the less you know the hotter you get."

101. Who said, "What you Kansas farmers ought to do is to raise less corn and raise more hell"?

102. A Danish theologian and philosopher combined his existential view of the world, "Life is not a problem to be solved but a reality to be experienced," with a commitment to the "leap of faith" — that it is "greater to believe, more blessed to contemplate the believer." Name him.

103. "But let there be spaces in your togetherness, /And let the winds of heaven dance between you." Where do we find these words of wisdom on marriage?

104. The epigraph to this book explains its title. "On the old highway maps of America, the main routes were red and the back roads blue. Now even the colors are changing. But in those brevities just before dawn and a little after dusk . . . they carry a mysterious cast of blue, and it's that time when the pull of the blue highway is strongest, when the open road is a beckoning, a strangeness, a place where a man can lose himself." What *is* the title and who is the author?

97. Anne Morrow Lindbergh

98. Jack Kerouac

99. Martin Luther King, Jr.

100. Bertrand Russell

101. Mary Lease (political speech, 1890)

102. Soren Kierkegaard

103. *The Prophet* (Kahlil Gibran)

104. *Blue Highways* by William Least Heat Moon

105. What ancient mathematician had the nerve to tell a ruler, "There is no royal road to geometry"?

106. She said, "It is better to die on your feet than to live on your knees." Name her.

107. We're all familiar with the expression, "Beauty is in the eye of the beholder." But who wrote it?

108. What American entertainer said, "Fifty million Frenchmen can't be wrong"? And what French novelist, critic, poet, and playwright observed, "If fifty million people say a foolish thing, it is still a foolish thing"?

109. Who said, "I am tired and sick of war. Its glory is all moonshine. . . . War is hell"?

110. Who said, "We must all hang together, or assuredly we shall all hang separately," and on what famous occasion did he say it?

111. What fictional characters took the words "All for one, one for all, that is our device" as their motto?

112. What poet said, "You don't have to suffer to be a poet. Adolescence is enough suffering for anyone"?

T*he real art of conversation is not only to say the right thing in the right place but to leave unsaid the wrong thing at the tempting moment.*

—Dorothy Nevill

105. Euclid (Proclus, *Commentaries on Euclid*, "Prologue")

106. Dolores Ibarruri (radio speech, July 18, 1936)

107. Margaret Wolfe Hungerford (*Molly Bawn*)

108. Texas Guinan thought they couldn't be wrong and Anatole France begged to differ

109. William T. Sherman

110. Benjamin Franklin, at the signing of the Declaration of Independence on July 4, 1776

111. The Three Musketeers (Alexandre Dumas)

112. John Ciardi

113. Who included in her autobiography this sad commentary on her early life: "At fifteen, life had taught me undeniably that surrender, in its place, was as honorable as resistance, especially if one had no choice"?

114. She wrote:

> "All things bright and beautiful
> All creatures great and small."

Name her.

115. Whose business philosophy was summed up in the line "There's a sucker born every minute"?

116. "Happiness is a warm puppy." Who wrote that?

117. Atticus described real courage to his children as being "when you know you're licked before you begin but you begin anyway and you see it through no matter what. You rarely win, but sometimes you do." From what novel does this come?

118. What twentieth-century statesman practiced what he preached? "Never look down to test the ground before taking your next step: only he who keeps his eye fixed on the far horizon will find his right road."

119. Clyde Edgerton wrote this in which of his novels? "People thought that time never stood still, . . . but she knew that for a minute before the sunrise when the sky began to lighten . . . there was often a pause when nothing moved, not even time, and she was always happy to be up and in that moment; sometimes she tried . . . to not move with time not moving, and it seemed that if she were not careful she might slip out of this world and into another."

120. Who wrote this tribute to Franklin Roosevelt? "The final test of a leader is that he leaves behind him in other men the conviction and the will to carry on."

113. Maya Angelou (*I Know Why the Caged Bird Sings*)

114. Mrs. Cecil Francis Alexander

115. P. T. Barnum

116. Charles Schulz (creator of the comic strip *Peanuts*)

117. *To Kill a Mockingbird* (Harper Lee)

118. Dag Hammarskjold (*Markings*)

119. *Walking Across Egypt*

120. Walter Lippmann

121. Horace Greeley included the famous words "Go West, young man, and grow up with the country" in an essay for *The New York Tribune*. He later credited another as the source for the line. Who was it?

122. Although the line "Neither rain, nor snow, nor heat, nor gloom of night keeps them from their appointed rounds" is commonly associated with letter carriers for the U.S. Postal Service today, it was originally applied to another group of messengers in the fifth century B.C. Who?

123. The words that have become the famous naval motto, "Don't give up the ship," are attributed to Captain James Mugford in 1776. However, Commodore Perry had them at the masthead of his flagship after the death of another heroic naval commander, who'd said, "Tell the men to fire faster and not to give up the ship." Who was this nineteenth-century officer?

124. Who wrote, "Character builds slowly, but it can be torn down with incredible swiftness"?

125. Who gave this extremely appropriate curtain speech — "That's all there is, there isn't any more"?

126. Who wrote, "Fame always brings loneliness. Success is as ice cold and lonely as the North Pole," in what novel?

127. Who observed that "life is the only sentence that doesn't end with a period"?

128. What humorist described man as "the only animal that blushes. Or needs to"?

E*ducation has produced a vast population able to read but unable to distinguish what is worth reading.*

— George M. Trevelyan

121. John Babsone

122. The couriers of Xerxes' Persian Empire (Herodotus [Book VIII]. The actual wording is "Not rain, no, nor snow, nor heat, nor night keeps them from accomplishing their appointed courses with all speed.")

123. Captain James Lawrence (killed on board the U.S. frigate Chesapeake in a naval engagement June 1, 1813)

124. Faith Baldwin ("July," *Harvest of Hope*)

125. Ethel Barrymore (at the conclusion of *Sunday*)

126. Vicki Baum in *Grand Hotel*

127. Lois Gould (*Such Good Friends*)

128. Mark Twain (*Pudd'nhead Wilson's New Calendar*)

Section Five

Characters

1. The characters are Robert Walton, Victor (an inventor), Justine, and The Monster. Give the title of the novel and its author's name.

2. Some of the characters in this Spanish novel are Dulcinea, Sancho Panza, Pedro Perez, and Samson Carrasco. Name the novel and its author.

3. Name the book whose characters include Frederic Henry, an American serving with an Italian ambulance unit; Catherine Barkley, an English nurse; and Rinaldi.

4. Who said, "Why don't you speak for yourself, John?" in what poem?

5. "Whenever they's a fight so hungry people can eat, I'll be there. . . . why, I'll be in the way guys yell when they're mad an' . . . I'll be in the way kids laugh when they're hungry an' they know supper's ready." Whose famous speech is this and in which Steinbeck novel does he appear?

6. The narrator and the title character of this poem by Edgar Allen Poe "loved with a love that was more than love." Name her.

7. Who was "exceedingly surprised with the print of a man's naked foot on the shore, which was very plain to be seen on the sand"?

8. Mrs. Wickett, Kathy Bridges, and the Brookfield boys are in this novel about a teacher in an English boys' school. What is the book?

All of my past life that has not faded into mist has passed through the filter, not of my mind, but of my affections.

—Iris Origo

1. *Frankenstein* by Mary Wollstonecraft Shelley

2. *Don Quixote* by Miguel Cervantes

3. *A Farewell to Arms* (Ernest Hemingway)

4. Priscilla Mullins in "The Courtship of Miles Standish" (Henry Wadsworth Longfellow)

5. Tom Joad, *The Grapes of Wrath*

6. Annabel Lee

7. Robinson Crusoe (*Robinson Crusoe*, Daniel Defoe)

8. *Goodbye, Mr. Chips* (James Hilton)

9. He's Savannah's and Luke's brother, the son of "a beautiful, word-struck mother" named Lila and a shrimper named Henry. Who is he?

10. Raskolnikov, a Russian student; Dounia, his sister; Sonia, a prostitute; Profiry, inspector of police; and Razumihin, friend of Raskolnikov all appear in what novel?

11. A hilarious eighteenth-century novel includes the characters Olivia Primrose, Sophia Primrose, George Primrose, Moses Primrose, Squire Thornhill, and Sir William Thornhill. What is its title?

12. Among the residents of Salem, Massachusetts, around 1850 are Miss Hepzibah Pyncheon, her brother Clifford, Judge Jaffrey Pyncheon, Phoebe Pyncheon, and Mr. Holgrave, Hepzibah's lodger, according to a very famous novel. Name the title and its author.

13. "I thought I loved Ashley who loved Melanie, so I married her brother Charles Hamilton. Later I married my sister Sue Ellen's beau Frank Kennedy because he had the money to save my home. But I never loved anyone but Rhett." Who am I?

14. In what epic do Priam, Hector, Helen, Paris, Menelaus, Agamemnon, and Achilles appear?

15. He was a "man with a mouth like a mastiff, a brow like a mountain, and eyes like burning anthracite." He beat "Old Scratch" himself in the biggest case of his life because even the damned had to salute his eloquence. What New Hampshire statesman is the main character in this Stephen Vincent Benet story?

16. What character in a James Whitcomb Riley poem has these lines:

> "An' the Gobble-uns 'at gits you
> Ef you—Don't—Watch—Out!"?

9. Tom Wingo in Pat Conroy's *The Prince of Tides*

10. *Crime and Punishment* (Fyodor Dostoyevsky)

11. *The Vicar of Wakefield* (Oliver Goldsmith)

12. *The House of the Seven Gables*, Nathaniel Hawthorne

13. Scarlett O'Hara in *Gone With the Wind* (Margaret Mitchell)

14. *The Iliad* (Homer)

15. Daniel Webster ("The Devil and Daniel Webster")

16. Little Orphant Annie

17. The story takes place in Kansas City, Chicago, and Lycurgus, New York. The characters include Clyde Griffiths, his mistress, Roberta, Clyde's wealthy uncle Samuel Griffiths, and Sondra Finchley, a society girl. Name the novel.

18. In what book do Christian, Faithful, Hopeful, Mr. Worldly Wiseman, Evangelist, Despair, Ignorance, and Apollyon appear?

19. Set in the Georgia back country of the 1920s, some of the characters are Jeeter, Ada, Pearl, and Ellie May Lester. Name the novel and its author.

20. Jake Barnes, a newspaperman; Lady Brett Ashley, one of the "lost generation"; Robert Cohn, a young writer; and Michael Campbell, Lady Brett's fiance, appear in a classic novel. Give the title and the author.

21. The central character of this novel is Carol Milford, wife of Dr. Will Kennicott in Gopher Prairie. In what novel does this unhappy housewife appear?

22. These characters appear in a Russian novel of social criticism — Count Vronsky, Stepan Oblonsky, Kitty Shtcherbatsky, and Konstantin Levin. What novel?

23. One of the most famous baseball players in the history of the sport is the "mighty Casey," who brought no joy to Mudville when he struck out. Who gave us the poem "Casey at the Bat"?

24. In which of Dickens' novels do the following characters appear: Anthony, his son Jonas, Seth Pecksniff, Mark Tapley, and Mrs. Sarah Gamp?

If a man does not keep pace with his companions, perhaps it is because he hears a different drummer.

—Henry David Thoreau

17. *An American Tragedy* (Theodore Dreiser)

18. *Pilgrim's Progress* (John Bunyan)

19. *Tobacco Road,* Erskine Caldwell

20. *The Sun Also Rises* (Ernest Hemingway)

21. *Main Street* (Sinclair Lewis)

22. *Anna Karenina* (Leo Tolstoy)

23. Ernest Lawrence Thayer

24. *Martin Chuzzlewit*

25. What nineteenth-century novel had these characters: Cedric the Saxon, Lady Rowena, Isaac of York, King Richard I, and Robin Hood?

26. Who created the character eulogized in these words: "You're a better man than I am, Gunga Din"?

27. The characters in this novel, later adapted as the movie *Apocalypse Now*, include Marlow and Mr. Kurtz. What is the novel and who's the author?

28. The action in this novel takes place 632 years after Ford, and the main characters are Bernard Marx, Lenine Crowne, John the savage, and Mustapha Mond (a World Controller). What is the title and who is the author?

29. For what group did Rudyard Kipling speak when he wrote that, although it's often " 'Chuck 'im out, the brute!' " in peace time, it's " 'Savior of 'is country'/ When the guns begin to shoot"?

30. Some of the characters in this French social satire are Cunegond, daughter of Baron Thunder-ten-tronckh, the tutor Pangloss, and a servant named Cacambo. What's the title?

31. We meet the characters of this novel in the scrub country of 1930s Florida. They are Jody Baxter; his father; Penny, his mother; Ora; and Flag—a fawn. What is the title and who is the author?

32. Identify the book from this cast of characters: a prisoner at Chateau d'If, Mercedes, Edmond Dantes, Abbe Faria, Ferdinand Mondego, and M. Danglers.

I am sitting in the smallest room in my house. I have your review in front of me. Soon it will be behind me.

—German composer Max Reger

25. *Ivanhoe* (Sir Walter Scott)

26. Rudyard Kipling ("Gunga Din")

27. *The Heart of Darkness* by Joseph Conrad

28. *Brave New World*, Aldous Huxley

29. The ordinary British soldier ("Tommy")

30. *Candide* (Voltaire)

31. *The Yearling*, Marjorie Kinnan Rawlings

32. *The Count of Monte Cristo* (Alexandre Dumas)

33. This epic novel set in the time of Christ has among its characters the Egyptian Balthasar, his daughter Iras, the Jewish merchant Simonides, his daughter Esther, and the Roman Messala. Name it and its author.

34. Can you identify the comic English novel in which Squire Allworthy, Bridget Allworthy, Jenny Jones, Captain Blifil, Sophia Western, and Molly Seagrim appear?

35. What nineteenth-century Russian novel has these characters: Dmitri, Ivan and Alyosha, the three sons of a profligate businessman; Grushenka, loved by both Dmitri and his father; Father Zossima, an aged priest; and Katerina, Dmitri's betrothed?

36. The scene is 1930s Tibet, and the characters are Hugh Conway, a British consul; Henry Barnard, an American embezzler; Miss Brainklow, a missionary; Chang, a Chinese Lama; and Father Perrault, the High Lama. Name the book.

37. After being pursued all his life by the relentless Javert, Jean Valjean saves his enemy's life when he could instead have killed him. In what novel do they appear?

38. In what book do these characters appear: Captain William Bligh, Roger Byam, Fletcher Christian, and Tehani (a Tahitian girl)?

39. During the course of a single day (June 16, 1904) in Dublin, we meet Stephen Dedalus, Leopold Bloom, Buck Mulligan, Mr. Deasy, Molly Bloom, and Gerty MacDowell. Name the novel in which they appear and its author.

40. Among the characters in this novel set during the Spanish Civil War are Robert Jordan, Pablo, Pilar, Maria, and Anselmo. What is the novel and who wrote it?

33. *Ben Hur*, Lew Wallace

34. *Tom Jones* (Henry Fielding)

35. *The Brothers Karamazov* (Fyodor Dostoyevsky)

36. *Lost Horizon* (James Hilton)

37. *Les Misérables* (Victor Hugo)

38. *Mutiny on the Bounty* (James Hall and Charles Nordhoff)

39. *Ulysses*, James Joyce

40. *For Whom the Bell Tolls*, Ernest Hemingway

41. One of Eudora Welty's most famous short stories describes Phoenix Jackson's long trip into Natchez to get medicine — a story in which the road she takes is also a character. What is the title of the story?

42. This author uses the theme of a relationship between two men, usually a pair quite different in makeup: Charly Bruno/Guy Haines in *Strangers on a Train* and Tom Ripley/ Frank Pierson in *The Boy Who Followed Ripley*, for example. Who is she?

43. Who traveled around the world in eighty days in the Jules Verne novel?

44. This novel takes place in fifteenth-century Paris; the characters are Quasimodo, Esmerelda, Claude Frolle, Phoebus de Chateaupers, and Gringoire. Give the title and the author.

45. Can you name the title or the author from this list of characters in the novel: Philip Carey, William Carey, Louisa Carey, Miss Wilkinson, Mildred Rogers, Thorpe Athelny, and Sally Athelny?

46. Who cried to the Confederate soldiers:

> "Shoot, if you must, this old gray head,
> But spare your country's flag"

in the poem by John Greenleaf Whittier?

47. Fictional characters like Coalhouse Walker mingle with such historical figures as Emma Goldman, Morgan, and Ford in this Doctorow tour de force. What's the title?

48. In Ken Follett's *The Eye of the Needle*, how did "Die Nadel" earn his nickname?

The more I see of men, the more I like dogs.

—Madame de Stael

41. "A Worn Path"

42. Patricia Highsmith

43. Phileas Fogg and Passepartout

44. Did the name Quasimodo ring a bell? If so, you know the novel is *The Hunchback of Notre Dame* by Victor Hugo.

45. *Of Human Bondage*, Somerset Maugham

46. Barbara Frietchie ("Barbara Frietchie")

47. *Ragtime*

48. From his favorite weapon, the stiletto

49. What famous fictional detective said, "When you have eliminated the impossible, whatever remains, however improbable, must be the truth"?

50. The characters in this Victorian novel include Pip, Pip's brother-in-law Joe Gargery, Miss Havisham, her ward Estella, Herbert Pocket, Mr. Jaggers, Mr. Provis, and Compeyson. Name the title and the author.

51. What American poet created the character who tells us that: "Father calls me William, sister calls me Will, Mother calls me Willie, but the fellers call me Bill!"?

52. In Emma Lazarus's poem, who says:

> "Send these, the homeless, tempest-tossed, to me:
> I lift my lamp beside the golden door."

53. What ruler of an unusual territory is "the roller of big cigars, / The muscular one" who whips "in kitchen cups concupiscent curds"?

54. In *Bread and Wine*, the integrity and courage of the revolutionary Pietro Spina stand in stark contrast to the widespread willingness to compromise with the fascists in Mussolini's Italy according to this author. Who is he?

55. The characters in this novel are Ishmael, Queequeg, Captain Ahab, Starbuck, and Stubb. In what novel do they appear? And who was the customs official who created them and their quarry based on his early experiences at sea?

56. In this novel set on a Civil War battlefield, we meet the young recruit Henry Fleming and the veterans Jim Conklin and Wilson. What is the title and who is the author of this classic work?

G*reat loves too must be endured.*

— Coco Chanel

49. Sherlock Holmes (*The Sign of Four*, Arthur Conan Doyle)

50. *Great Expectations*, Charles Dickens

51. Eugene Field

52. The Statue of Liberty ("The New Colossus")

53. The Emperor of Ice Cream (Wallace Stevens, "The Emperor of Ice Cream")

54. Ignazio Silone

55. *Moby Dick*, Herman Melville

56. *The Red Badge of Courage*, Stephen Crane

57. Can you identify the book and its author from this cast of characters: Wang Lung, O-Lan, Lotus Blossom, Pear Blossom, Nung En, Nung Wen, and The Fool?

58. The characters in this satire on Victorian manners and morals include Becky Sharp, Amelia Sedley, Miss Crawley, Rawdon Crawley, George Osborne, and Captain Dobbin. Name the novel or the author.

59. Who described himself as "the master of fantasy" in *Une Saison en Enfer* (*A Season in Hell*), a psychological autobiography in prose-poem form?

60. Name the creator of such vivid characters as Beth and Wanda (*Small Change*), Vida (*Vida*), and Jill (*Braided Lives*).

61. Aunt Polly, Sid, Injun Joe, and Joe Harper are among the characters in this nineteenth-century novel set along the Mississippi River. Name the title character who convinces his friends to whitewash a fence for him.

62. In what Christmas classic do Ebeneezer Scrooge, Bob Cratchit, Jacob Marley, and Tiny Tim appear?

63. The characters of this novel set in New York City and on Long Island are Nick Carraway, Daisy and Tom Buchanan, and Myrtle Wilson. Name the title character and his creator.

64. What is the name of the character Tennyson described as the "lily maid of Astolat"?

No man knows his true character until he has run out of gas, purchased something on the installment plan, and raised an adolescent.

—Mercelene Cox

57. *The Good Earth*, Pearl Buck

58. *Vanity Fair*, William Thackeray

59. Arthur Rimbaud

60. Marge Piercy

61. Tom Sawyer (*Tom Sawyer*, Mark Twain)

62. *A Christmas Carol* (Charles Dickens)

63. Jay Gatsby (*The Great Gatsby*), F. Scott Fitzgerald

64. Elaine (*The Idylls of the King*)

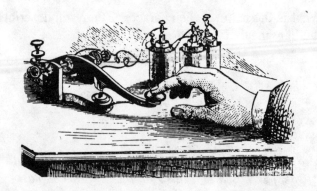

65. *Spoon River Anthology* consists of a series of poetic monologues by 244 former inhabitants of the area where the author spent much of his boyhood. Who is he?

66. Who is the ghost who walks at midnight:

> "A bronzed, lank man! His suit of ancient black,
> A famous high top hat and plain worn shawl,"

in Vachel Lindsay's poem?

67. The cast of characters include Maxim de Winter, the owner of Manderley and his second wife (who narrates the tale), Mrs. Danvers, Frank Crawley, and Jack Favell. Name the title character.

68. Although we hear more about this character than any other in *1984*, we never see him. Who is always "watching you"?

69. Danny Dalehouse, Marge Menninger, Nan Dimitrova, Muskrat Greencloud An-Guyen, and Kris Kristianides are among the characters in this story of colonizing a new planet. In what novel do they appear and who wrote it?

70. Spider Elliott, Valentine O'Neill, Wilhelmina Hunnewell Winthrop, and Vito Orsini are just a few of the characters who move in and out of a shopper's fantasy-come-to-life on Rodeo Drive. What's the name of the store (also the title of the book)?

71. Lois Lenski won the Newbery Medal for her portrait of Birdie Boyer, who belonged to a large "strawberry family" and dreamed of an education that included playing the organ. Name the book where we meet Birdie.

72. In what three novels does Erica Jong's Isadora Wing appear?

L*ess is more.*

—Mies van der Rohe

65. Edgar Lee Masters

66. Abraham Lincoln ("Abraham Lincoln Walks at Midnight")

67. Rebecca (*Rebecca*, Daphne du Maurier)

68. Big Brother (George Orwell)

69. *Jem*, Frederik Pohl

70. *Scruples* (Judith Krantz)

71. *Strawberry Girl*

72. *Fear of Flying, How to Save Your Own Life*, and *Parachutes and Kisses*

73. What classic children's story has the characters Master Cherry, Geppetto, and a Good Fairy?

74. Some of the characters in this novel set on the moors of England are Mr. Earnshaw, Catherine, Hindley, Heathcliff, Mr. Linton, and Mr. Lockwood. Name the book and the author.

75. Match the fates of the five children in Roald Dahl's *Charlie and the Chocolate Factory* with their names:

    1. Augustus Gloop
    2. Veruca Salt
    3. Violet Beauregard
    4. Mike Teaveed
    5. Charlie Buckett

    a. Will inherit the chocolate factory
    b. Goes up a pipe into the fudge room
    c. Turns into a blueberry
    d. Sent down to incinerator as a "bad nut"
    e. Shrunk when traveling via television

76. Although many of John Barth's early books had anti-heroes — Todd Andrews, Jake Horner, and Ebenezer Cooke — these give way to a genuinely heroic protagonist in which of his novels?

77. Among the wide assortment of characters in this novel are schoolteachers, wrestlers, radicals, Jenny Fields and her son, Helen, Harrison and Alice Fletcher, and Jillsy Sloper. What's the novel's title?

78. In which John Hersey novel do the following appear: Major Victor Joppolo, Sergeant Borth, Captain Purvis, Giuseppe, and Tomasino?

79. In what epic poem do Penelope, Telemachus, Calypso, and Circe appear, as well as various Greek gods and goddesses?

80. The main characters in the novel are Mrs. March, Jo, Meg, Beth, and Amy. Give the title and author.

73. *Pinocchio* (Collodi)

74. *Wuthering Heights*, Emily Brontë

75. 1., b.; 2., d.; 3., c.; 4., e.; 5., a.

76. *Giles Goat Boy; or a Revised New Syllabus*

77. *The World According to Garp* (John Irving)

78. *A Bell for Adano*

79. *The Odyssey* (Homer)

80. *Little Women*, Louisa May Alcott

81. In which of Ann Beattie's novels do we meet "Cindi Coeur," who writes hilarious letters to and from the love-lorn for *Country Daze*?

82. In this sentimental story written to protest cruelty to animals, the title character tells us about a happy childhood, followed by being sold farther and farther down the social scale. Finally rescued by Joe, he ends his days in clover. Who is this animal hero?

83. Why was Philip Nolan "The Man Without a Country" in the Everett Edward Hale story?

84. He was lame and stammered, ridiculed by his family, but he got the last word with his "tell-all" book about his grandmother Livia, Livia's son Tiberius, Germanicus, and Caligula. Who was he?

85. Who "flies through the air with the greatest of ease"?

86. The main characters in this comic novel about love and marriage are Mr. and Mrs. Bennet, their five daughters, Mr. Bingley, and Mr. Darcy. What is the title and who wrote it?

87. The hero of this bestseller by Ayn Rand, a conceited architect who justifies his faith in honest design by the end of the novel, is supposedly modeled on Frank Lloyd Wright. What's the novel's title?

88. Ross Murdock and Dr. Gordon Ashe travel back in time to the Bronze Age, through space, and into the future on a different planet in a series of popular science fiction novels for young people. Name the author.

"Realistic people" who pursue "practical aims" are rarely as realistic and practical, in the long run of life, as the dreamers who pursue their dreams.

—Hans Selye

81. *Love Always*

82. *Black Beauty* (Anna Sewell)

83. At his trial for treason, he said he never wanted to hear the name of his country again. The judge made that his sentence, and, for fifty-five years he never sets foot on land or hears or reads of the United States.

84. The Emperor Claudius (as drawn by Robert Graves in *I, Claudius*)

85. The daring young man on the flying trapeze (in the song by George Leybourne)

86. *Pride and Prejudice*, Jane Austen

87. *The Fountainhead*

88. Andre Norton (There are three novels about this pair: *The Time Traders*, *Galactic Derelict*, and *Key Out of Time*.)

89. Among the creations of this Venezuelan novelist and political leader are a barbaric female landlord (*Dona Barbara*), an illegitimate son seeking his family's acceptance (*La trepadora*), and a wandering minstrel (*Cantaclero*). Name this author, who was president of Venezuela before being deposed by Jimenez.

90. Few have "played" more roles in novels than a Louisiana politician who is the prototype for "Chuck" Crawford in *Number One*, Hank Martin in *A Lion Is in the Streets*, Gilgo Slade in *Sun in Capricorn*, Willie Stark in *All the King's Men*, and "Buzz" Windrip in *It Can't Happen Here*. Name the real person.

91. In what novel do Jane, Mrs. Reed, Bessie Leaven, Edward Rochester, and St. John Rivers appear?

92. Who created the characters Hester Prynne, her child Pearl, Arthur Dimmesdale, and Roger Chillingworth?

93. She is best known for her short stories, such as "Bliss" and "The Garden Party." But she's also a character in her own right, Gudrun in D. H. Lawrence's *Women in Love* and Beatrice Gilray in Aldous Huxley's *Point Counter Point*. Name her.

94. Who were archy and mehitabel?

95. Philomena Guinea in Sylvia Plath's *The Bell Jar* is a cruel caricature of the real benefactor who endowed Plath's Smith College scholarship and paid for her treatment following Plath's first suicide attempt. What is her benefactor's real name?

96. Who wrote a poem that describes seven "real cool" pool players at the Golden Shovel—who will probably die soon?

To speak ill of others is a dishonest way
of praising ourselves.

—Will and Ariel Durant

89. Romulo Gallegos

90. Huey Long

91. *Jane Eyre* (Charlotte Brontë)

92. Nathaniel Hawthorne (*The Scarlet Letter*)

93. Katherine Mansfield

94. The cockroach and cat created by Don Marquis

95. Olive Higgins Prouty (who wrote *Stella Dallas*, among other popular novels)

96. Gwendolyn Brooks ("We Real Cool")

97. Mr. Bumble, Mr. Brownlow, Mrs. Maylie, Rose Maylie, Fagin, Bill Sykes, and Nancy are just a few of the characters who appear in this Victorian novel. Name it and its author.

98. In what story does Ichabod Crane appear? And who is the author?

99. "Twelve and five-sixths years old," she was a "member of nothing in the world." Her name was Frankie and she did a lot of growing up the summer her brother got married. In what novel do we find her?

100. Name the character who appeared in all of the following: *Call for the Dead*; *Tinker, Tailor, Soldier, Spy*; and *The Honourable Schoolboy*.

101. Who described Saint Valentine as:

> "A gentleman, it's safe to say,
> Who owned a sense of humor,"

for having his day in unpleasant mid-February in her poem, "Poor Timing."

102. In the Walter de la Mare poem, "Silver," who slowly, silently "walks the night in her silver shoon"?

103. Some characters in this book, part of which is set in Transylvania, are Van Helsing, Jonathan Harker, Mina Murray, Lucy Westenra, Quincy Morris, Lord Godalming, and Dr. Seward. Name the author.

104. "I loved living in the mountains with my grandfather, and Peter, and the goats. But they made me live in the city so I could go to school. I felt so closed in that I started sleepwalking. Finally Clara and I came back to the mountains, where she began to walk again." Who am I?

R*osiness is not a worse windowpane than gloomy gray when viewing the world.*

— Grace Paley

97. *Oliver Twist*, Charles Dickens

98. "The Legend of Sleepy Hollow," Washington Irving

99. *Member of the Wedding*, Carson McCullers

100. John Le Carré's George Smiley

101. Phyllis McGinley

102. The moon

103. Bram Stoker (*Dracula*)

104. Heidi

105. What is Madame Bovary's first name?

106. He gave us some of the most famous characters in popular fiction, including Rosie and Charlie Allnutt in *The African Queen* and Captain Horatio Hornblower (series of novels). Who was he?

107. "My first instructor was Dr. Chandra. He taught me to sing a song, it goes like this 'Daisy, Daisy, give me your answer, do. I'm half crazy all for the love of you.' " These are virtually the last words he spoke to Dave. Who is he and in what book does he appear?

108. Name the author of many bestselling fictional biographies whose "characters" include Vincent Van Gogh (*Lust for Life*), Jack London (*Sailor on Horseback*), and Mary Todd Lincoln (*Love is Eternal*).

109. They first met in *Strong Poison* when she was on trial, accused of murdering her lover. They got engaged in *Gaudy Night*, and married in *Busman's Honeymoon*. Who are they?

110. This beloved author of children's books brought such lively individuals as Janey, the middle Moffat, and Ginger Pye. What's the name of this former children's librarian?

111. Name the English writer and illustrator who created such characters as Squirrel Nutkin and Jemima Puddleduck?

112. Pooh, Piglet, Rabbit, and Christopher Robin appear in two classic books by A. A. Milne. Give their titles.

E*instein was a man who could ask immensely simple questions. And what his work showed is that when the answers are simple too, then you can hear God thinking.*

—Jacob Bronowski

105. Emma (*Madame Bovary*, Gustave Flaubert)

106. C. S. Forester

107. HAL the computer in *2001: A Space Odyssey* (Arthur C. Clarke)

108. Irving Stone

109. Harriet Vane and Lord Peter Wimsey (creations of Dorothy Sayers)

110. Eleanor Estes

111. Beatrix Potter (perhaps best known for *The Tale of Peter Rabbit*)

112. *Winnie-the-Pooh* and *The House at Pooh Corner*

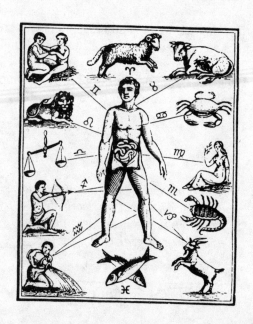

113. In what novel do we meet Hazel, Fiver, Buckthorn, Bigwig, Silver, and Bluebell?

114. In a famous poem, who came "riding-riding-riding, up to the old inn-door" to see "the landlord's black-eyed daughter/Bess, the landlord's daughter"?

115. This novel traces the lives of Vassar graduates Kay Strong, Priss, Libby, Norine Schmittlapp Blake, Dottie, Helena, Lakey, and Polly, who move in and out of each other's lives long after graduation. Name the novel and its author.

116. Who created the blond, teen-age (and ageless) girl detective whose companions include her lawyer father, their housekeeper, her cousins George and Bess, and sometime boyfriend, Ned Nickerson?

117. This amateur detective appeared in three of Poe's stories. His unofficially assisting the police, explaining to a bewildered friend, and use of cold logic became a model for many later literary detectives. Name him and one of the stories in which he appears.

118. In an unusual twist, his former publisher sued the author who created Jack Ryan, claiming the publisher and not the author had the rights to the character. Name the author, who *did* win in court and stayed with his new publisher, and the novel in which Ryan first appeared.

119. The prototype of this James Clavell character was an English navigator named William Adams. He remained in Japan after being detained while serving in the Dutch fleet in 1600 and married into Japanese aristocracy. Name the character and the novel in which he appears.

120. The title of this novel by Kingsley Amis is ironic since the story is about the comic *misfortunes* of the title character, a young, lower-middle class instructor at an English university. What's the novel's title? (Hint: The character's last name is Dixon.)

113. *Watership Down* (Richard Adams)

114. "The Highwayman" (Alfred Noyes)

115. *The Group*, Mary McCarthy

116. Carolyn Keene (Nancy Drew)

117. C. Auguste Dupin in *The Murders in the Rue Morgue, The Murder of Marie Roget*, and *The Purloined Letter*

118. Tom Clancy, *The Hunt for Red October*

119. John Blackthorne, *Shogun*

120. *Lucky Jim*

121. "Black Michael," the beautiful Princess Flavia, the dangerous rogue Rupert, the faithful Fritz and Colonel Sapt, and two identical cousins both named Rudolf are trapped in a web of romantic intrigue in Ruritania. In what novel?

122. In which of Arthur Hailey's novels do Warren Trent, Christine Francis, Peter McDermott, Dodo Lash, and Keycase Milne appear?

123. Rat, Mole, Toad, Badger, and a gang of unsavory stoats populate this children's classic. What's the title?

124. Assisted by his loyal secretary Della Street and private investigator Paul Drake, this trial lawyer consistently snatched courtroom victories from Hamilton Burger and confounded Lt. Tragg. Give his name and that of the author who invented him.

125. This martini-drinking spy who drives an Aston Martin loaded with unusual options is actually named after an ornithologist. Who is he, and who created him?

126. Among the characters in this novel by Gore Vidal are Salmon Chase, William Seward, Mr. and Mrs. Ben Helm, General McClellan, and "The Tycoon" and "The Hellcat" ("Madam" when she's in a good mood). Who are the two historical characters to whom John Hay gave these nicknames in the book?

127. Sethe kills her child to keep her from being returned to slavery — an act that continues to haunt her years later. Who created this tragic woman and in what novel do we find her?

128. These tales use animal characters to illustrate human foibles, like the original dog in the manger or the tortoise and the hare. By what title is this collection of stories generally known?

121. *The Prisoner of Zenda* (Anthony Hope)

122. *Hotel*

123. *The Wind in the Willow* (Kenneth Grahame)

124. Perry Mason, created by Erle Stanley Gardner

125. James Bond, created by Ian Fleming

126. Abraham and Mary Todd Lincoln (in the novel, *Lincoln*)

127. Toni Morrison, *Beloved*

128. *Aesop's Fables*

Section Six

Etc.

1. Often a political slogan becomes the "keynote" of an administration. Whose slogan was: "This nation, this generation, in this hour has man's first chance to build a Great Society"?

2. On August 25, 1944, Hitler asked the field commander on the spot, "Is Paris burning?" Was it?

3. This eighteenth-century French philosopher's writings made a profound impression on early American leaders and our Constitution. One such example is his, "I disapprove of what you say, but I will defend to the death your right to say it." Who was he?

4. What ancient Greek philosopher made this remark (some would say it's just as true today): "When there is an income tax, the just man will pay more and the unjust less on the same amount of income"?

5. Developments in the late 1980s suggest his fellow countrymen may no longer agree with the leader who said, "Whether you like it or not, history is on our side." Name him.

6. A man had a special room where he did all his research and writing; he decorated it all in red, from the ceiling to the floor. His friends said it reminded them of a famous detective story. Which one?

7. Who said, "I shall return," and where did he want to return to?

8. What is the correct punctuation of William Sydney Porter's pen name: O. Henry or O'Henry?

A*bstract Art: A product of the untalented, sold by the unprincipled to the utterly bewildered.*

—cartoonist Al Capp

1. Lyndon Baines Johnson

2. No

3. Voltaire

4. Plato, *The Republic*

5. Nikita S. Khrushchev

6. "A Study in Scarlet" (Arthur Conan Doyle)

7. Douglas MacArthur, on leaving Corregidor for Australia, March 11, 1942. He planned to return to the Philippines after driving the Japanese out.

8. O. Henry

9. In which of his novels did Anthony Burgess create a new language to evoke the violent lower-class teen subculture of his anti-hero, Alex?

10. Who said, "I am not an Athenian or a Greek, but a citizen of the World"?

11. What novel is subtitled "The White Whale"?

12. Once there was a director who lined up a number of men dressed in armor, to select one for a part in a play. He rejected the first eleven and picked the twelfth. Reminds you of the title of which Shakespearean play?

13. What Anglo-Irish dramatist said, "An Englishman thinks he is moral when he is only uncomfortable"?

14. What English novel of 1740 has the subtitle, "or, Virtue Rewarded"?

15. What notable eighteenth-century personality said, "I would rather be attacked than unnoticed. For the worst thing you can do to an author is to be silent as to his works"?

16. We usually refer to it as *Dr. Jekyll and Mr. Hyde*. What's the full title?

Man is not the sum of what he has but the totality of what he does not yet have, of what he might have.

—Jean-Paul Sartre

9. *A Clockwork Orange*

10. Socrates (From Plutarch, *Of Banishment*)

11. *Moby Dick* by Herman Melville

12. *Twelfth (K)Night*

13. George Bernard Shaw (*Man and Superman*)

14. *Pamela* (Samuel Richardson)

15. Samuel Johnson (Boswell's *Life of Johnson*)

16. *The Strange Case of Dr. Jekyll and Mr. Hyde* (Robert Louis Stevenson)

17. Identify the American raconteur, journalist, and critic who said, "I must get out of these wet clothes and into a dry Martini"?

18. What is the title of the classic children's novel with the subtitle "or Adventures on a Desert Island"?

19. Who was the ancient Greek who, legend reports, became so excited by a discovery made in his bathtub that he ran naked through the streets of Syracuse crying, "Eureka, eureka"?

20. Whose administration is associated with the phrase "The New Frontier"?

21. Identify the Polish astronomer who said, "Finally we shall place the sun himself at the center of the Universe."

22. What poet rearranged history when he wrote:

    "Or like stout Cortez when with eagle eyes
    He stared at the Pacific"?

23. A very popular nineteenth-century novel was subtitled "A Tale of the Christ." What's the title?

24. What line of poetry follows this: "When Adam delved and Eve span"?

Nobody sees a flower — really — it is so small — we haven't time — and to see takes time like to have a friend takes time.

— Georgia O'Keeffe

17. Alexander Woolcott

18. *Swiss Family Robinson* (Johan Wyss)

19. Archimedes, because while in his bath, he had identified the principles behind the displacement of water

20. John F. Kennedy (from a line in his inaugural address, "The New Frontier of which I speak is not a set of promises — it is a set of challenges")

21. Nicolaus Copernicus (*De Revolutionibus Orbium Coelestium*)

22. John Keats ("On First Looking into Chapman's Homer")

23. *Ben Hur* (Lew Wallace)

24. "Who was then the gentleman?" (attributed to John Ball during the Wat Tyler Rebellion)

25. One of this author's characters said, "He had used the word in its Pickwickian sense." Who was the author?

26. Who was the American ɪ̇ndustrialist who said, "History is more or less bunk"?

27. What is the *full* title of Gibbon's famous history of the Roman Empire?

28. Which English religious leader said he "looked upon the world as my parish"?

29. Very few people know this, but some of the immigrants who landed at Plymouth set out immediately for Disneyland in California. They kept a trip diary, carefully recording the number of miles they traveled each day, etc. What did they call this diary?

30. What American admiral sent this radio message after the Japanese had reported sinking all his ships: "Our ships have been salvaged and are retiring at high speed toward the Japanese fleet"?

31. What sixteenth century Italian political observer wrote, "Whoever desires to found a state and give it laws, must start with assuming that all men are bad and ever ready to display their vicious nature"?

32. The title of this Daniel Defoe novel begins with the words *The Life and Strange and Surprising Adventures of*. What's the rest (and more famous part) of it?

T*rue friendship comes when silence between two people is comfortable.*

—Dave Tyson Gentry

25. Charles Dickens (*The Pickwick Papers*)

26. Henry Ford

27. *The History of the Decline and Fall of the Roman Empire*

28. John Wesley

29. Pilgrim's Progress

30. Admiral W. F. Halsey

31. Niccolo Machiavelli (*The Prince*)

32. *Robinson Crusoe* (the full title is: *The Life and Strange and Surprising Adventures of Robinson Crusoe, of York, Mariner*)

33. It was a good thing he thought he'd "rather be right than be President," because he never did get elected. What nineteenth-century American statesman ran for president three times without success?

34. What nineteenth-century British prime minister dismissed a fellow politician as "A sophistical rhetorician, inebriated with the exuberance of his own verbosity"?

35. What was the pen name of Herman Cyril McNeile (an English crime and adventure writer), and what's the name of his most famous character, a sort of modern Robin Hood?

36. What Frenchman said, "The way to be a bore is to say everything"?

37. What Roman boasted, "I found Rome a city of bricks and left it a city of marble"?

38. What philosopher offered this sage advice, "Govern a great nation as you would cook a small fish — don't overdo it"?

39. Thomas Hardy's novel, *Far From the Madding Crowd*, takes its title from this line of poetry: "Far from the madding crowd's ignoble strife." Name the poem it comes from and the poet.

40. Who issued the following warning as a prologue to one of his books: "Persons attempting to find a motive in this narrative will be prosecuted; persons attempting to find a moral in it will be banished; persons attempting to find a plot in it will be shot"?

*Life can only be understood backwards;
but it must be lived forwards.*

—Soren Kierkegaard

33. Henry Clay

34. Benjamin Disraeli (speech at Knightsbridge on July 27, 1878)

35. Under the pen name "Sapper," McNeile created Bulldog Drummond

36. Voltaire (*Sept Discours en Vers Sur l'Homme*)

37. Augustus Caesar (Suetonius, *Augustus*)

38. Lao Tzu (*The Way*)

39. "Elegy Written in a Country Churchyard," Thomas Gray

40. Mark Twain ("By Order of the Author," *Huckleberry Finn*)

41. What influential American novel first published in 1852 had the subtitle *"Or, Life Among the Lowly"*?

42. Name the Roman writer who coined the phrase "bread and circuses."

43. Who said, "I have nothing to offer but blood, toil, tears and sweat"?

44. What Roman senator ended every one of his political speeches with the words *"Cartago delenda est"* and what did he want?

45. Who said, "When we say 'the state,' the state it is we, it is the proletariat, it is the advance guard of the working class"?

46. The subtitle of this book is *And What Alice Found There*. What's the title?

47. What is the title of an 1861 English novel subtitled *The Weaver of Raveloe*?

48. In what poem do we find the sensible business advice, "Ah, take the Cash, and let the Credit go"?

If someone gives you so-called good advice, do the opposite; you can be sure it will be the right thing nine out of ten times.

—Anselm Feuerbach

41. *Uncle Tom's Cabin* (Harriet Beecher Stowe)

42. Juvenal (*Satires, X*)

43. Winston Churchill (in his first statement to the House of Commons as prime minister, May 13, 1940)

44. Marcus Porcius Cato (Cato the Elder), "Carthage must be destroyed"

45. Nikolai Lenin

46. *Through the Looking Glass* (Lewis Carroll)

47. *Silas Marner* (George Eliot)

48. *The Rubiyat of Omar Khayyam* (Edward FitzGerald, translator)

49. What holiday is associated with the poem that begins "Should auld acquaintance be forgot" and who wrote it?

50. Who wrote the poem immortalized in song by the gentlemen songsters of Yale that includes the lines "We're poor little lambs who've lost our way"?

51. Which Soviet leader said, "A single death is a tragedy, a million deaths is a statistic"?

52. "For the second time in our history, a British prime minister has returned from Germany bringing peace with honour. I believe it is peace for our time." To what event did the prime minister refer—and was he right?

53. What American journalist wrote about the experience of combat in World War II from "the worm's-eye point of view"?

54. What World War I officer described his situation in this oddly optimistic way: "My center is giving way, my right is in retreat; situation excellent, I shall attack"?

55. What city did O. Henry describe as "Baghdad on the Subway"?

56. Who coined the phrase "the lost generation" and to what group is it generally applied?

No one can make you feel inferior
without your consent.

—Eleanor Roosevelt

49. New Year's Eve; the poet is Robert Burns ("Auld Lang Syne")

50. Rudyard Kipling ("Gentlemen Rankers")

51. Joseph Stalin

52. Unfortunately for him, Neville Chamberlain was wrong about the success of the Munich Conference with Hitler. War came a short time later.

53. Ernie Pyle (*Here is Your War*)

54. Marshal Ferdinand Foch (Second Battle of the Marne, 1918)

55. New York ("The Discounters of Money" in *Roads of Destiny*)

56. Gertrude Stein (Hemingway used it as an epigraph for *The Sun Also Rises*) to describe the American expatriates in Europe in the 1920s

57. What famous architect is buried in St. Paul's Cathedral with the epitaph "If you would see my monument, look around"?

58. This line of poetry from *The Rubiyat* reads, "I sometimes think that never blows so red/The Rose as where some buried Caesar bled." It inspired the title for a Rex Stout novel. Who, or what, was the buried Caesar in the case?

59. On the eve of which war did Edward, Viscount Gray say, "The lamps are going out all over Europe; we shall not see them lit again in our lifetime"?

60. What colorful children's book has sold more copies than any other?

61. Who said, "Doctor Livingstone, I presume?" and what was his occupation?

62. This song, which includes the line "Weep no more, my lady," is played at a famous horse race every year. What is its title and who wrote it?

63. Which French king felt "Paris is well worth a Mass," and why did he say it?

64. At the height of Star Trek's original popularity, buttons reading "I grok Spock" were everywhere. But the word "grok" didn't come from the series. Name the book it did come from and the author.

T*he new electronic independence recreates the world in the image of a global village.*

—Marshall McLuhan

57. Sir Christopher Wren

58. A pedigreed bull

59. World War I

60. Dr. Seuss's *Green Eggs and Ham* (5,000,000+)

61. Henry Stanley, a journalist

62. "My Old Kentucky Home" by Stephen Collins Foster (played at the Kentucky Derby)

63. Henry IV referring to the fact that he would have to convert to Catholicism in order to ascend the throne

64. *Stranger in a Strange Land*, Robert Heinlein

65. What book did Richard Wright, noted author of *Native Son* and *Black Boy*, describe as having been his "literary Bible" for many years?

66. Before becoming a disciple of the "confessional" poetic school of Robert Lowell and W. D. Snodgrass, what career did Anne Sexton pursue?

67. What twentieth-century rebel and social reformer said, "Nonviolence and truth are inseparable and presuppose one another. There is no god higher than truth"?

68. The term "natural selection" is part of what scientific theory, and who developed it?

69. What was Oliver Wendell Holmes protesting when he wrote, "Ay, tear her tattered ensign down"?

70. William Carlos Williams wrote many poems celebrating the perception of the extraordinary in the ordinary. In his best known poem, on what simple object does so much depend?

71. Of which of her contemporaries did Margaret Fuller say, "smokes, wears male attire, wishes to be addressed as Mon frere; perhaps if she found those who were as brothers indeed, she would not care whether she were a brother or sister."

72. What actress did Dorothy Parker describe like this, "She runs the gamut of emotions from A to B"?

S*ome problems never get solved. They just get older.*

—Chaim Weizmann

65. H. L. Mencken's *Book of Prefaces*

66. She was a fashion model

67. Mohandas K. Gandhi (*True Patriotism: Some Sayings of Mohatma Gandhi*)

68. Evolution, Charles Darwin (*The Origin of Species*)

69. The navy's plan to scrap the U.S.S. Constitution ("Old Ironsides"). The poem aroused public opinion and the ship was saved.

70. A red wheelbarrow ("The Red Wheelbarrow")

71. George Sand (Amandine Aurore Lucile Dupin, as famous for her affairs as her writing)

72. Katharine Hepburn

73. What American humorist said, "All I know is just what I read in the papers"?

74. He used his real name, Charles Lutwidge Dodgson, on the mathematical discourses he wrote, but a pen name on some charming fantasies for young people. What was his pen name?

75. One of America's most respected men of letters, he has received the National Book Award, the Pulitzer Prize, and the Bollingen Prize in Poetry. In 1986 he was chosen America's first poet laureate. Name this distinguished writer.

76. In her ground-breaking book, this feminist wrote, "A mystique does not compel its own acceptance." Who is she and what's the title of the book?

77. One of Japan's most prolific authors (*Forbidden Colors* and *The Sailor Who Fell From Grace with the Sea* among others) committed suicide in 1970 after an unsuccessful demonstration against Japan's weak military position. The leader of the Shield Society, dedicated to restoring the ideals of the samurai to modern society, died true to those ideals. Who was he?

78. With what two sports is author Ring Lardner most often associated?

79. What was Diogenes looking for when he roamed the streets in broad daylight carrying a lantern?

80. His theory of population, which bears his name, is summed up in these lines "Population, when unchecked, increases in a geometrical ratio. Subsistence only increases in an arithmetical ratio." Name this sociologist.

W*e have met the enemy and it is us!*

—Pogo

73. Will Rogers

74. Lewis Carroll (*Alice in Wonderland* and *Through the Looking Glass*)

75. Robert Penn Warren

76. Betty Friedan, *The Feminine Mystique*

77. Yukio Mishima

78. Baseball and boxing

79. An honest man

80. Thomas Malthus; he propounded the "Malthusian Doctrine" in his treatise, *An Essay on Population*

81. The author wrote his book to promote the cause of social-
    ism, and it derives its power from his anger over the social
    injustices of the meat-packing industry. The book is more
    famous, however, for having prompted Theodore Roose-
    velt to initiate food inspection laws. What's the book's title
    and who wrote it?

82. Every American history pupil knows that Charles Pinck-
    ney defied Talleyrand's bribe-seeking agents with the
    words "Millions for defense but not one cent for tribute."
    Did he?

83. What is the title of the novel one of the characters is writing
    in Andre Gide's *The Counterfeiters*?

84. In addition to detailing the lives of his characters, John Dos
    Passos used three techniques — "the Newsreel," "the
    Camera Eye," and biographies of public figures — to make
    this trilogy a wide panorama of national life. Can you name
    all three titles, or at least the name of the whole trilogy?

85. What American politician is associated with the adage
    "Speak softly and carry a big stick"?

86. What rather humorless English queen pronounced, "We
    are not amused"?

87. A book often described as the "most famous book that
    never existed" appears frequently in the horror stories of
    H. P. Lovecraft. What is its title and who supposedly wrote
    it?

88. In Ursula Le Guin's *The Word for World Is Forest*, who are
    the brutal invaders of the beautiful, peaceful planet?

T*reat your friends as you do your pictures,*
and place them in their best light.

—Jennie Jerome Churchill

81. *The Jungle*, Upton Sinclair

82. Not exactly. He actually said, "No, no, not a penny."

83. *The Counterfeiters*

84. The individual titles are *The 42nd Parallel*, *Nineteen Nineteen*, and *The Big Money*; the trilogy is called *U.S.A.*

85. Theodore Roosevelt

86. Queen Victoria (the remark appears in *Notebooks of a Spinster Lady* and was supposedly uttered when Victoria encountered a member of her household doing an imitation of her majesty's imperious ways)

87. *The Necronomicon* of the Mad Arab Abdul Alhazred

88. People from Earth (us, in other words)

89. Then there was the fellow who took wonderful care of his car. He loved it so much that, when it finally died, he wrote a book titled *The Life of a Car*. His wife, however, suggested a much better title. What was it?

90. Who invented the cinquain: a five-line poem with two syllables in the first line, four in the second, six in the third, eight in the fourth, and a drop back to two in the last?

91. His line "Experience keeps a dear school, but fools will learn in no other" might have been applied to one of his experiments with a kite — but he escaped without injury. Who was he?

92. To what historic event do the words "That's one small step for a man, one giant leap for mankind" refer and who said them?

93. Notorious in its time for the author's sexual ideas, today this autobiographical novel is considered most significant for its piercing psychological insight into the Oedipal relationship between mother and son — and a complex web between mother and son and son and other woman. Who was the "real" Paul Morel and what's the title of the novel?

94. Often called "the last of the gentle saints," this country clergyman wrote subtle, introspective poems exploring faith and man's life with God. However, most people who've met his works in a literature class remember him for two poems written in shapes that reflects their subjects: "Altar" and "Easter Wings." Name him.

95. A famous novelist served as a war correspondent from 1938 to 1941 with an equally famous photographer, who also happened to be his wife. Name this talented (but incompatible) couple.

96. Although he's best known for his primary genre, the short story, this Argentinian also produced poetry, essays, and Spanish translations of Gide, Melville, Faulkner, and Kafka. Name him.

89. *Autobiography*

90. Adelaide Crapsey

91. Benjamin Franklin (*Poor Richard's Almanac*)

92. Man first setting foot on the moon (July 20, 1969), Neil Armstrong

93. D. H. Lawrence, *Sons and Lovers*

94. George Herbert

95. Erskine Caldwell and Margaret Bourke-White

96. Jorge Luis Borges

97. Who said, of the Battle of Britain, ". . . and so bear our-
    selves that, if the British Empire and its commonwealth
    last for a thousand years, men will still say 'This was their
    finest hour' "?

98. What city did Ernest Hemingway describe as a "moveable
    feast"?

99. The trilogy—*The Man of Property*, *In Chancery*, and *To
    Let*—traces an upper-middle class English family from the
    Victorian age to the period between the wars. By what
    name is the whole trilogy known?

100. In the story "The Invisible Man" by G. K. Chesterton,
     Father Brown and Flambeau investigate a murder commit-
     ted by a man who entered and left a building seemingly
     unseen by eight human eyes. But he wasn't really invisible
     at all. What made him "mentally invisible" so everyone
     looked but never saw him?

101. Over how many days does the mystery unfold in Umberto
     Eco's *The Name of the Rose*? And what should that remind
     us of?

102. Joyce Carol Oates was nominated three times for the Na-
     tional Book Award before she won. Which book finally won
     her the award: *Expensive People*, *A Garden of Earthly De-
     lights* or *Them*?

103. Who said, "There is such a thing as a man being too proud
     to fight"?

104. Who made history by saying, "Mr. Watson, come here, I
     want you"?

F or fiction, imaginative work that is, is not dropped
like a pebble upon the ground, as science may be;
fiction is like a spider's web, attached ever so lightly
perhaps, but still attached to life at all four corners.

—Virginia Woolf

97. Winston Churchill

98. Paris (the entire epigraph to *A Moveable Feast* reads, "If you are lucky enough to have lived in Paris as a young man, then wherever you go for the rest of your life, it stays with you, for Paris is a moveable feast")

99. *The Forsyte Saga* (John Galsworthy)

100. He was the mailman, and carried out the body in his bag!

101. Seven days: seven days of destruction which mirrors the seven days in which the Creation took place, according to *Genesis*

102. *Them*

103. Woodrow Wilson

104. Alexander Graham Bell (the first time a message was successfully sent by telephone)

105. "The Queen of Romance Fiction" is related to a future queen as well—Diana, Princess of Wales. Name this royal writer who has written hundreds of historical romances featuring virtuous heroines and romantic, often rather rakish, noblemen?

106. The inspiration for her finest novel came from the prairie town of Red Cloud, Nebraska, where she lived from age ten through sixteen. Who immortalized both Annie Pavelka, the model for the title character, Antonia, and her farmhouse?

107. What was the title of the story about a broken traffic light?

108. Although he realized his first literary successes as a poet, we know him better for his novels *Beulah Land* and the Pulitzer-Prize-winning *Honey in the Horn*. Who is he?

109. Ernest Hemingway's *For Whom the Bell Tolls* takes its title from this line of poetry: "Therefore never send to know for whom the bell tolls; It tolls for thee."

Who wrote the poem?

110. Who said, "That this nation, under God, shall have a new birth of freedom"?

111. Who are commemorated by Tennyson's lines "Theirs not to reason why/Theirs but to do or die," and what did they do?

112. Currer, Ellis, and Acton Bell were used as pseudonyms by a trio of women writers in the nineteenth century. They're now known by their real names; what are they? (Hint: They were the daughters of a clergyman and had a brother named Patrick Branwell.)

There's a period of life when we swallow a knowledge of ourselves and it becomes either good or sour inside.

—Pearl Bailey

105. Barbara Cartland

106. Willa Cather (*My Antonia*)

107. *Forever Amber* (the original best-selling novel about a pro-miscuous Restoration beauty was written by Kathleen Winsor)

108. H. L. Davis

109. John Donne (*Devotions XII*)

110. Abraham Lincoln ("The Gettysburg Address")

111. The poem, "The Charge of Light Brigade" celebrates the Light Brigade, who knew the folly of their orders but charged into certain death on the Russian line during the Battle of Balaclava

112. Charlotte, Emily, and Anne Brontë—in that order

113. In this novel, an unfinished literary property is left as an ambivalent bequest to a man who is satirized in it but nevertheless makes a good deal of money from it. What's the title of the novel and who wrote it?

114. Which of Matthew Arnold's poems is a memorable expression of a late nineteenth-century belief that the "Sea of Faith," at high tide in an earlier time, was now rapidly ebbing?

115. What is the term for the poetic device Poe employs in "The Bells" when he writes of "the tintinnabulation . . . of the bells, bells, bells"?

116. "Or The Wonderful Lamp" is the subtitle of a classic story. What is the title?

117. Mary Ann Evans used a pen name. What was it?

118. Anyone who is crazy can be grounded; all he has to do is ask. But if he asks, he can't possibly be crazy—request refused. What's the term for this circular bureaucratic formula and who used it as a title for a novel?

119. What form does the narrative take in Alice Walker's *The Color Purple*?

120. Who translated this and what was the original language:

> "Oh. Threats of Hell and Hopes of Paradise!
> One Thing at least certain—this life flies"?

T o love what you do and feel that it matters—
how could anything be more fun?

—Katharine Graham

113. *Humboldt's Gift*, Saul Bellow

114. "Dover Beach"

115. Onomatopoeia

116. "Aladdin"

117. George Eliot

118. Catch-22, Joseph Heller

119. Celie's letters to God and to her sister

120. Edward FitzGerald is the original translator from Persian of *The Rubiyat of Omar Khayyam*

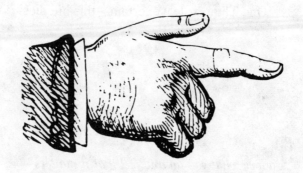

121. Name the American imagist poet arrested for treason because of his pro-Mussolini radio broadcasts.

122. A great modern novel begins with the memories triggered by the taste of a madeleine soaked in tea. Whose memories were these?

123. Matsuo Basho is generally acknowledged as the developer and master of a form of poetry composed of seventeen syllables giving a complete impression or mood. What is this form called?

124. Many people find this short story upsetting—it shows children stoning their own mother to death after a ritual lottery whose meaning is long forgotten. The point, of course, is that people shouldn't kill other people, any people, for any reason. Who wrote this very effective story and what's the title?

125. What was the pen name of music hall dancer and mime turned author Sidonie Gabrielle Claudine Colette Goudelet?

126. What do *The Mists of Avalon, The Hollow Hills,* and *The Once and Future King* all have in common?

127. Name the Civil War prison commemorated in the Pulitzer-Prize-winning book that bears its name written by McKinley Kantor.

128. What poet wrote the poem that captures a marching rhythm with the line "Boots—boots—boots—boots—movin' up and down again!"?

You give but little when you give of your possessions. It is when you give of yourself that you truly give.

—Kahlil Gibran

121. Ezra Pound

122. Marcel Proust (*Remembrance of Things Past*)

123. Haiku

124. Shirley Jackson, "The Lottery"

125. Colette (remember *Gigi?*)

126. All are retellings of the Arthurian legend (Marion Zimmer Bradley wrote *The Mists of Avalon*, Mary Stewart, *The Hollow Hills*, and T. H. White, *The Once and Future King*)

127. Andersonville

128. Rudyard Kipling ("Boots")

Index